William K. Quick

SIGNS OF OUR TIMES

A Vision for the Church

Abingdon Press
Nashville

SIGNS OF OUR TIMES
A Vision for the Church

Copyright © 1989 by Abingdon Press

Second Printing 1989

Library of Congress Cataloging-in-Publication Data

QUICK, WILLIAM K. (WILLIAM KELLON), 1933—
Signs of our times / William K. Quick.
p. cm.
ISBN 0-687-38449-4 (alk. paper)
1. Sermons, American. 2. United Methodist Church (U.S.)—Sermons. 3. Methodist Church—Sermons. I. Title.
BX8333.Q48S54   1989
252'.076—dc19   88-28622
                                                          CIP

Scripture quotations unless otherwise noted are from the Revised Standard Version of the Bible, copyright 1946, 1952, 1971 by the Division of Christian Education of the National Council of the Churches of Christ in the USA, and used by permission.

Those noted NEB are from The New English Bible. © The Delegates of the Oxford University Press and The Syndics of the Cambridge University Press 1961, 1970, Reprinted by permission.

Those noted TLB are from *The Living Bible*, copyright © 1971 by Tyndale House Publishers, Wheaton, IL. Used by permission.

Those noted MLB are from the *Modern Language Bible: The Berkley Version in Modern English*. Copyright © 1945, 1959, 1969 by Zondervan Publishing House. Used by permission.

Those noted Phillips are from the New Testament in Modern English, copyright © by J. B. Phillips 1958, 1960, 1972.

Those noted Goodspeed are from (The Complete Bible: An American Translation, translated by J. M. P. Smith and Edgar Goodspeed).

Those designated GNB are from the Good News Bible—Old Testament: Copyright © American Bible Society 1976; New Testament: Copyright © American Bible Society 1966, 1971, 1976.

Those noted KJV are from the King James Version of the Bible.

Those noted JB are from The Jerusalem Bible, copyright © 1966 by Darton, Longman & Todd, Ltd. and Doubleday & Company, Inc. Used by permission of the publisher.

Those noted NKJV are from The New King James Version. Copyright © 1979, 1980, 1982, Thomas Nelson Inc., Publishers.

MANUFACTURED BY THE PARTHENON PRESS AT NASHVILLE, TENNESSEE, UNITED STATES OF AMERICA

To

Stephen Kellon, Kathryn Elizabeth
David Christopher and *Paul Sanders Quick*

In whose lives
I see signs of hope for our times
and
In whose love
Is mirrored the image of the eternal God
—ever giving and forgiving!

Acknowledgments

I would embark upon an impossible task if I sought to name those whose lives, insights, and counsel over these thirty-five years have helped shape my preaching ministry. From the days of Dean James Cleland, preaching professor at Duke Divinity School, and Carl J. Sanders during his dynamic ministry at Broad Street Church in Richmond, to this present time I have been inspired by a multitude of great preachers. I disagree with those who view preaching as an outmoded form of communication. The eternal Word does come to life through the spoken Word and I have known those moments when a strange silence welded together a whole congregation and a new grasp of the Good News united us in joyous faith.

There are those, however, to whom a special word of thanks is due for this 1989 United Methodist sermon series on The Protestant Hour and I would be remiss without thanking them.

To the United Methodist Communications (UMCOM) committee which chose me for this rare privilege, I am grateful. A preacher is chosen every third year, in rotation with the Southeastern and South Central Jurisdictions, by UMCOM and this pastor has been so honored.

In the midst of my preparation for this series, we were saddened and shocked by the sudden death of David Abernathy, whose name became synonymous with the Protestant Radio and Television Center (PRT) in Atlanta and with The Protestant Hour across the nation. On April 11, 1988, David joined the Church Triumphant. Along with a number of ministers, I owe an incalculable debt to David. He was a brilliant and talented communicator and consistently brought the highest standards of broadcasting to The Protestant Hour. His was a combination of rare gifts and graces. There was a nobility in David that enriched the lives of all whom he touched. In truth we shall not see his like again.

To William (Bill) Horlock and the technical staff of the PRTC, I am grateful for their tireless work in recording the 1989 series.

Thanks are due my Metropolitan Church family in Detroit, the parish clergy and lay staff for their second-mile efforts in ministry during the weeks of preparation. Wallace Hamilton, one of my pulpit mentors, was granted a three-month period, free of parish responsibility, to write his sermon series for The Protestant Hour. I now know why!

Among those who deserve a special word are Bishop H. Hasbrouck Hughes, Jr., a colleague from Randolph-Macon and Duke days; to Donn Michael Farris, Divinity School librarian at Duke and his staff; to Dr. William E. Smith, Stanley Sutton and Parker Duncan; to my wife Barbara, for adjusting family schedules; and to Virginia Conrad for secretarial assistance during the research and writing.

A special tribute to Mary I. Levack, whose editing skills, counsel, and deep insights into the Christian faith and journey, brought the manuscript through many revisions.

Finally, my heart overflows with gratitude to Jesus and the Christ who called this poor servant to the holy task of "proclaiming the Good News" and to those long-suffering congregations in Richmond, Virginia, Morehead City, Bahama, Zebulon, Greenville and Durham, North Carolina, and in Detroit who have nurtured and encouraged us during these years. In these churches preacher and community have shared a common life and I can only trust that the faith within each congregation has been aroused, strengthened, and deepened.

To that same end, I offer the radio congregation of The Protestant Hour, the current series.

Bill Quick
Metropolitan Church
Detroit, Michigan
September 1988

Contents

Introduction

Jesus said one should know how to distinguish "the signs of the times" (Matt. 16:4 Phillips).

Since childhood, I have been fascinated with jingles and slogans. Advertisers seize upon them to peddle their products; the demand for sales in our consumer-oriented society and the creative ingenuity of Madison Avenue have spawned firms with multimillion dollar accounts.

All of us know the signs of the times made popular by radio and television advertising with catchy tunes and memorable slogans. A major automobile manufacturer tells us to "listen to the heartbeat of America." A soft drink ad insists that "the real thing" is their cola. We listen, of course, but in our thoughtful moments, we are nagged with the notion that America's hearbeat is more than an automobile and that "the real thing" cannot be found at a soda fountain or in a bottle.

Nor are the "signs of the times" limited to commercial advertising. Churches and some Christians have had a series of religious slogans burned into their consciousness: "Prepare to meet God," "Jesus is coming soon," "Prayer changes things," "Where will you spend eternity?" All of these are among the visible signs of the times.

Many people reject the religious slogans as the work of the overzealous or the fanatical. Others seize upon them as the perfect expression of their bumper-sticker theology.

The church is called on to evaluate the signs of the times, both sacred and profane. It is our task to search for authenticity in those signs and slogans that proport to do God's work in our midst. God's Word is contemporary. God speaks to us through the needs of each generation and with each generation's technology, through the signs of our times. It is our job to be sure that the voice that is heard is that of the real God, and not of the huckster.

More and more I have come to realize that the contemporary church must be the agency that directs modern humanity away from the pitchman and back to the eternal God. "For it is Christ Jesus as Lord whom we preach, not ourselves; we are your servants for Jesus' sake. God, who first ordered light to shine in darkness, has flooded our hearts with his light, so that we now can enlighten men with knowledge of the glory of God, as we see it in the face of Christ" (II Cor. 4:5-6 Phillips). This Christ must be "the heartbeat of America . . . and the world!" because this Christ is "the real thing."

The story that we must tell—and those slogans, properly interpreted, can help us do it—is that the work of God becomes incarnate in the hearts of men and women by faith in Christ and in the doing of his work in our daily lives. It has become increasingly easy in the late twentieth century to adulterate the faith and twist the gospel to fit the times. When we allow that to go unchallenged, we make it easy for the sloganeers and salespeople. With apologies to the ancient economist, in the currency of the mind, bad ideas must not be allowed to drive out the good.

This series of sermons is an attempt to get underneath some of the confusion resulting from popular religious slogans and the fads instigated by media advertising. To evaluate the signs of our times is to judge them in light of the gospel. The endeavor to interpret them in that way may be repugnant to fundamentalists and confusing to radicals, but it is welcomed by the overwhelming number of Americans who seek something more lasting than fads and more penetrating than slogans. The crisis in the church today is at heart a biblical and theological crisis born in an era of pop culture and pop religion and nurtured by the neglect of the Gospels and Christian apologetics. The crisis will remain until we choose whom to believe: Jesus Christ or the con-artist.

It is my hope that you will find fresh insight in this attempt to interpret the signs of the times in light of the gospel. It will, I trust, help you resolve some of the confusion that exists in American life today. Viewed in light of the gospel, those slogans become powerful reminders of our need for a closer, personal relationship with the living Lord.

The promise is ours and it is eternal: "I will make a new covenant. . . . I will put my law within them, and I will write it upon their heart" (Jer. 31:31-33).

The signs that I covet for myself and the church are those written on our hearts, not those worn on a lapel, stuck on a bumper, or plastered on a billboard. While each of those signs delivers a message, the message most often takes us away from the truth rather than toward it. The answer to the contemporary problem is not to be found in a jingle or a slogan. The answer is to be found in a faith so authentic, so human, so convincing that the only one who can explain it is Jesus Christ.

William K. Quick
Metropolitan Church
Detroit, Michigan

LENT

Forty lean days
Crossed by six Sabbaths
Beginning in ashes,
Ending in Life.

Bernard Via, Jr.

After this Joseph of Arimathea, who was a disciple of Jesus, but secretly, for fear of the Jews, asked Pilate that he might take away the body of Jesus, and Pilate gave him leave. So he came and took away his body. Nicodemus also, who had at first come to him by night, came bringing a mixture of myrrh and aloes, about a hundred pounds' weight. They took the body of Jesus and bound it in linen cloths with the spices, as is the burial custom of the Jews. Now in the place where he was crucified there was a garden, and in the garden a new tomb where no one had ever been laid. So because of the Jewish day of Preparation, as the tomb was close at hand, they laid Jesus there **(John 19:38-42).**

Come Out of the Closet!

"Come out of the closet" is a cry being heard across the country. I want to seize upon this phrase as a plea to those whom I choose to label "closeted Christians." It is a call to those followers of Jesus whose identity in the world has been, for practical purposes, secretive or covered up. Come out of the closet and reveal your faith to your world: to neighbors and friends, to associates and fellowworkers—the faith you claim as your Christian orientation. The church today suffers from an identity crisis exemplified by those followers of Jesus who could claim the central figure in today's sermon, Joseph of Arimathea, as their patron saint.

All four Gospels tell us about Joseph. Mark says he was "a respected member of the Council . . . who looked forward to the kingdom of God" (Mark 15:43 NEB). Matthew tells us he was rich, for he "was a man of means, and had himself become a disciple of Jesus" (Matt. 27:57 NEB). Luke is more revealing and tells us he was "a good, upright man" (Luke 23:50 NEB). John, however, explicitly reveals him to be a closeted Christian, "a disciple of Jesus, but a secret disciple for fear of the Jews" (John 19:38 NEB).

This is a rather strange scene, John relates. The body of a criminal customarily was not buried. It was left to be consumed by vultures. Jesus' body was saved from that indignity. Joseph approached Pilate and asked if he might be allowed to remove the body of Jesus. He was joined by a compatriot—a like-minded and good-intentioned fellow member of the Sanhedrin, Nicodemus, who had first visited Jesus by night. Pilate granted permission and the two men took the carpenter-preacher's body and buried it in Joseph's new tomb. Intriguing, this cameo from Golgotha!

Luke tells us Joseph and Nicodemus did not agree with the Sanhedrin's verdict or the sentence imposed on Jesus by that court, so their faith now moved them into action. They took the body from the cross, anointed it with expensive perfumes, and wrapped it with strips of linen cloth. Then they carried Jesus' body to a rock-hewn tomb never before used for a burial.

Let us be thankful for what they did. They came forward and gave Jesus a fitting burial. Without Joseph and Nicodemus, Jesus' body might have been the food of vultures.

On the other hand, how sad to have waited until a loved one died to honor him! Loyalty in life and flowers for the living are worth far more than accolades and wreaths for the dead. A word of love and appreciation goes farther in life than glowing tributes paid over a dead body.

I find it a sad commentary on both Joseph and Nicodemus that their names are not mentioned in the book of Acts, the biblical account that tells us who the first Christians were and what they did to establish the church.

Perhaps they had personal reasons for their secret discipleship. John says Joseph was "fearful." We assume, had he declared his discipleship, his position in the Sanhedrin would have been jeopardized.

Our discipleship, however, is seldom called into question. More often than not it is indiscernible if not invisible. So, how do we justify our closeted religion?

America is not an irreligious country. The national polls tell us that 94 percent of the American people believe in God; 87 percent say they pray, and 60 million adults profess to have been "born again." Over a hundred million people worship in our churches on Sunday. There is no shortage of divine sentiment, but our religion is divorced from our daily life.

The greatest divorce of the twentieth century has been the divorce between the sanctuary and the marketplace. The marketplace sued the sanctuary for its irrelevance in daily life.

On Sunday we worship together in gorgeous cathedrals, stately churches, picturesque chapels, and on Monday we are back in the marketplace going our separate ways. One finds it difficult to tell who at the office, in the factory, at the bank had acknowledged God on Sunday. During the week, little difference is visible between the worshiper and the non-worshiper. Evil seems to be more zealous in spreading perversion than, good is in bearing witness to faith and in seeking conversion.

Is life today any different than it was in biblical times?

The gospel tells of a Pharisee who went to the Temple to recite to God all the good things he did: how often he fasted and what big checks he wrote to community charities. He boasted about his prayer life and was proud that he was not like those who were not religious.

Today the church has little need to worry about modern-day pharisees making a show of their religion. The Pharisee in the Bible wanted everybody to know how good he was. The modern pharisee is not inclined to let anyone know! We have become closeted Christians.

Is there any wonder that the unbeliever may be excused for saying, "If his faith means so little to him in business or to her in social life or in conversation, how could it make any difference in my life?"

At times I wonder if there isn't a deeper spiritual yearning among those who profess no religion than there is among those who profess it on Sunday and ignore it during the week. If those of us blessed with faith care not to share it or even show it, should we be surprised that the spiritually starved are looking everywhere else—even outside the church for something or someone to believe in and to worship?

Some seek it in bizarre cults or religious sects, while others seek it in a political ideology, right or left. They yearn for something to believe in and to which they can commit their lives. Others seek it in sex—not because it satisfies but because it brings an intensity at the moment that enables them to forget the purpose and value of life. Anything can fill up the void created when faith is gone.

Bumper-sticker theology is a prevalent sign of our times. On a Detroit freeway one trucker's witness raises a curious question: "If you were accused in court of being a Christian, would there be enough evidence to convict you?" Ponder that question as it relates to you! Could your wife, husband, or children give evidence that your faith is really authentic in your household? Might a colleague from work take the witness stand on your behalf to testify that your faith is evident in that arena? Would your monthly bank statement reflect your Christian "faith commitment"? Jesus did say, "Where your treasure is, there will your heart be also" (Matt. 6:21 KJV).

Often pastors are asked, "Is so-and-so a member of your church?" One pastor responded, "The name is on our church roll but I cannot really say he or she is a member." Every congregation has church members whose case would be dismissed in a court of law because of insufficient evidence to prove they were Christians.

A Scandinavian churchman came to work in North Carolina. He searched for reasonable lodging. Answering an ad that offered a room at an affordable rate, he found it had a peculiar requirement: "The renter must be a regular church-goer." He assured the landlady that he met the condition so he moved in. A

month later he still had not attended worship any-
where. When the landlady confronted him with his
negligence and reminded him of his pledge, he assured
her he was a man of his word. "How do you account for
the fact that you've slept in every Sunday and have yet
to darken the door of a house of God?" He protested, "I
go to church regularly! Always have! Regularly! Every
Christmas and every Easter!" The fellow reminds me of
the woman who complained that her church was in a
rut because every time she went there they had a
Christmas tree up!

Some people, sadly, could never be convicted of being
church members. Somewhere along the way, they have,
like Joseph, come to know Jesus. Attracted to Christ,
Joseph became a disciple—"but secretly." Some day he
would come out in the open, but Mark says he "waited."
Perhaps later!

Perhaps you have been "waiting," thinking a more
opportune time will come. May I suggest that today is
the time. It is the beginning of Lent.

Lent is a time when the real you and the real me are
called to self-examination and self-discipline in the
presence of the Lord. We are encouraged to journey
inward to face our true selves, discover our strengths,
admit our weaknesses, and determine, by God's grace,
to change whatever needs to be changed. Then and there
we begin to grow in his grace, more than ever aware that
we are his beloved, forgiven children. Many Christians
treasure Lent for this reason.

There is, however, a great danger that the whole
tradition of Lent can be only an exercise in window-
dressing—just a show—or a time of mock discipline
which leaves our deep inner being unscathed.

The danger we are in, even those of us who attend
church regularly, is that we see the Christian life as
living in such a manner that our neighbors will be
impressed. It sometimes appears that we may be more
concerned to impress our friends than we are to invite

God deep into the recesses of our souls to work there his miracle of love and grace. If we're that concerned with appearance, then the truth is: God cannot win the world until he has first won us!

Joseph of Arimathea was concerned with appearance. He could not jeopardize his standing with his friends. He could not run the risk of losing credibility or station in life. Why are we so obsessed with appearance? Our response to Christ is to be prompted from within our hearts—not by how other people see us. God knows who and what we are. Not even a face-lift or designer clothes will prohibit God from seeing beyond our appearance to the heart of who we are.

Christians who desire to move beyond appearance and to come out of the closet need a model. We have a model! His name is Jesus.

Jesus grew up in the hill country of Galilee. He left his carpentry bench in Nazareth to become an itinerant preacher. A profoundly religious Jew, he questioned and moved beyond his Jewish heritage. Faithful to the synagogue, he spent his weekdays in the marketplace. Faithful to his Jewish world, he went into the forbidden territory of Samaria. Faithful to the Old Testament Law, he reflects the joy and spontaneity of grace.

Without a single trace of self-consciousness, Jesus ate with sinners and often found them closer to the truth than their religious counterparts—arrogant in their self-righteousness. He found that his enemies were the establishment of his day. The priests and the politicians, for the sake of religion and the nation, wanted him dead. Jesus was challenged, tried, and executed by people who saw in him a threat to their influence and power. Spread-eagled and hammered to a wooden cross between two thieves, Jesus died for the sins of us all.

This is our model: the Son of God who asks us to "come out of he closet," to open our lives to him and to witness to the world *who* we are and *whose* we are. This is the God who calls us to open our hearts to him.

The question is, Will we? Dare we trust him? Think not what we might lose if we come out of the closet but rather what we will gain. The evangel of love speaks to us. His promise is:

"Fear not, I am with thee; O be not dismayed,
For I am thy God, and will still give thee aid;
I'll strengthen thee, help thee, and cause thee to stand,
Upheld by my righteous, omnipotent hand.

"The soul that on Jesus still leans for repose,
I will not, I will not desert to his foes;
That soul, though all hell should endeavor to shake,
I'll never, no, never, no, never forsake!"

God's promise is still true. But some don't know that! Some lack the courage to believe. Some fear what others may say or think. Many hearts ache, yearning to be what God destined them to become. They tire of putting on an act for their friends. The promise of God given to the church at Corinth by Paul is our promise, "No eye has seen, nor ear has heard, neither has the human heart thought of what God has prepared for those who love Him" (I Cor. 2:9 MLB). This is the promise. This is the invitation: "Come out of the closet!"

A colleague of mine with whom I discussed this message raised a probing thought for Christians who need to come out of the closet. She offered the revealing insight: "Perhaps that cannot happen until they first 'go into the closet!' " Is this a word from the Lord?

Jesus, in the Sermon on the Mount, invited his listeners to do precisely that. Speaking of prayer, Jesus told his hearers, "When thou prayest, enter into thy closet, and when thou hast shut thy door, pray to the Father which is in secret; and thy Father which seeth in secret shall reward thee openly" (Matt. 6:6 KJV).

The depths of Jesus' life was grounded in his private prayer life. He prayed at ever turn, on any occasion.

Anthony Padovano reminds us that:

He prays . . . each day, during the night, while on the water, lost in the mountains, alone in the temple, forsaken in the garden, at supper with his friends, throughout the ordeal of the cross. He prays not to teach us a lesson or because it is something one must, after all, do. Jesus prays because he believes. . . . He prays because his Father needs trust, his enemies need love, his friends need his presence, his heart needs grace, his family needs community, his existence needs redemption, his life needs a purpose.[1]

Jesus' public witness is a matter of public record. Read the Gospels: Matthew, Mark, Luke, and John. Jesus' inner strength was anchored in his relationship with his Father. Whatever his need, he took it to the Lord in prayer. Jesus emerged from those times renewed, refreshed, empowered.

Jesus was never hesitant to make the journey into his closet.

Dag Hammarskjöld once called the longest journey, "the journey inward" to the center of your being. Are you and I reluctant to take that journey? It may lead us to change something in our lives or, more important, to change something within ourselves.

Jesus is our model!

Perhaps he holds the secret. Christ may be calling us, you and me, nominal Christians or otherwise, to "go into our closet" before we can hope to "come out of the closet!"

Now the tax collectors and sinners were all drawing near to hear him. And the Pharisees and the scribes murmured, saying, "This man receives sinners and eats with them." . . .

"There was a man who had two sons; and the younger of them said to his father, 'Father, give me the share of property that falls to me.' And he divided his living between them. Not many days later, the younger son gathered all he had and took his journey into a far country, and there he squandered his property in loose living. And when he had spent everything, a great famine arose in that country, and he began to be in want. So he went and joined himself to one of the citizens of that country, who sent him into his fields to feed swine. And he would gladly have fed on the pods that the swine ate; and no one gave him anything. But when he came to himself he said, 'How many of my father's hired servants have bread enough and to spare, but I perish here with hunger! I will arise and go to my father, and I will say to him, "Father, I have sinned against heaven and before you; I am no longer worthy to be called your son; treat me as one of your hired servants." ' And he arose and came to his father. But while he was yet at a distance, his father saw him and had compassion, and ran and embraced him and kissed him. And the son said to him, 'Father, I have sinned against heaven and before you; I am no longer worthy to be called your son.' But the father said to his servants, 'Bring quickly the best robe, and put it on him; and put a ring on his hand, and shoes on his feet; and bring the fatted calf and kill it, and let us eat and make merry; for this my son was dead, and is alive again; he was lost, and is found.' And they began to make merry **(Luke 15:1-3, 11-24).**

Lost and Found!

A few years ago I was preaching on a Sunday morning in the great auditorium of the Ocean Grove Camp Meeting on the Jersey Shore. When I read the Scripture lesson and the congregation learned that the morning sermon was on the prodigal son, three thousand faces became a sea of smiles. When I returned to my seat following the reading, the camp meeting president leaned over and said, "You're the fourth consecutive minister this summer to preach on the prodigal son!"

As I began the sermon, I said to the crowd—not eager, I am sure, to hear yet another sermon on the topic—"I suppose that some of you feel like the fellow who said, 'I've heard the story of the prodigal son preached from every point of view except that of the pigs.' " I assured them that this sermon would not come from that perspective, and they settled in with support for the visiting preacher who had been caught totally unaware.

Parables are simple stories meant to shed welcome light on moral and spiritual truth rather than sacred riddles to be solved. The parables of the lost sheep, the lost coin, and the lost son are stories for every generation. They speak to us of Jesus' interest in all areas of human concern. However, we learn here that Jesus has a passionate concern for the lost. These incomparable stories—so well known and so dearly loved—contain the very heart of the good news Jesus came to tell. So familiar and comfortable are they that we must not lose sight that they are true and striking pictures of our Lord's interest in everything that is *lost*.

What did Jesus mean by "the lost"? Something is lost if its owner cannot enjoy or properly make use of it. A coin is lost when it can't be used as currency. A sheep is lost if it has wandered away from the care and watchful eye of its shepherd. A son is lost when he wanders away from the loving, caring fellowship of his parents. People are "lost" when they are not fulfilling their true purpose in life, in service to and in fellowship with their Creator.

Among the most tender and beautiful biblical stories are these wherein Jesus tells us what it is to be "lost and found."

The first two parables, "the wandering sheep" and "the lost coin," were spoken by Jesus in response to those who grumbled at his friendly social relations with sinners. The scribes and Pharisees mumbled, "He receives and eats with sinners." Who were these sinners? The publicans and the lawbreakers.

The publicans were more than internal revenue types employed by their own government. They were Jews working as tax collectors for Rome. They were despised by their own people and considered traitors! The sinners, or people of the land as they were known, were Jews who did not keep the Jewish law. The Pharisees had a regulation for dealing with such sinners.

> "When a man is one of the People of the Land, entrust no money to him, take no testimony from him, trust him with no secret, do not appoint him guardian of an orphan, do not make him the custodian of charitable funds, do not accompany him on a journey."[1]

The Pharisee, or religious man, was forbidden by law to have any business dealings with such a person whether it be buying or selling. He was forbidden even to receive a sinner into his home. The Pharisees were shocked that Jesus not only had personal contact with sinners but that he also ate with them. How scandalous! This outrageous man receives sinners and eats with them!

The rabbis taught that repentant sinners would be welcomed by God. But Jesus is saying in these parables that God does not wait for sinners to return to him. He is saying that God goes in search of them and rejoices when they are found, as did the shepherd, the householder, and the father. The point of these stories is that the shepherd went in search of the lost sheep, the woman searched for the lost coin, and the prodigal, of his own free will, came home to a father who, having kept an open door waiting for his return, ran to meet him.

These parables were told chiefly for the benefit of the Pharisees and scribes. Perhaps Jesus was trying to help them understand that self-righteous persons, such as themselves, who thought they did not need repentance, were badly mistaken. It is not only the world's prodigals who are in need of God's acceptance. The spiritual prodigals need it too.

The nineteenth-century reformer Wendell Phillips was traveling on a train one day. As he sat quietly reading, a somewhat zealous and brash stranger poked a religious tract into his hands and said, "My business is saving souls from hell." Phillips, without looking up, replied, "Then I'd suggest that you go there and attend to your business." It was a fully deserved rebuke. Too often we religious people set ourselves up as judge and jury of all who are different from us. Are we then like the Pharisees? If so, the stories are intended for us as well as for those who heard them first from Jesus.

The focus of this sermon, however, centers not on the lost sheep or the lost coin but on what some have called the greatest short story in the world. It is a story about a man with two sons. The main point of the story is that the grace of God is bestowed as freely on the rebellious younger son as on his faithful elder brother, regardless of merit. No story from the Gospels needs less interpretation than this matchless parable of man's folly and God's love. In terms completely simple and profoundly moving God's concern for the lost is set forth.

Here is a younger brother: bright, quick, restless, fed up with a confining home life. He wants to be free, out from under, to go find, and do his thing. "To be sure," he says, "I won't find it here. The old man gets on my nerves. Don't do this and don't do that. I'm tired of this dead place, doing boring chores, fighting dumb rules, and besides, nobody understands me!"

He must have been aware, at least, of the Jewish law that said a father was not free to distribute his property as he chose. Under the law, the elder son must get two-thirds and the younger, one-third (Deut. 21:17). The boy and his father must have talked about such matters. Surely the father was aware of his independent, headstrong, bored rascal and his unhappiness. So he was not shocked when the boy demanded, "Father, give me my part of the property coming to me anyway. I'm clearing out." The father said not a word. He knew he had already lost this boy and he would not stand in his way. He had enough good sense not to try to force him to stay at home. He got the money and gave the boy his share of the inheritance.

The father, wounded, fearful, and anxious, stood at the door and watched him leave. Will he ever come back?

Life can only be understood backward, but it has to be lived forward, without benefit of hindsight.

"Give me!" the son said. His thought is all of himself and his claims on others—not at all of their claims on him. Give me—my share!

So he packed up and went away. Luke doesn't tell us where. Just far enough from home, from his father's house, his family, his country to be free and enjoy life. He was adventurous. He was climbing a fool's hill. He didn't think far ahead and hadn't much of an idea of what to do but enjoy himself. He didn't invest any of the inheritance; he didn't even use it; he squandered it!

With reckless prodigality, self-centered and indifferent to the claims of others, he indulged himself and loved it! The dough from home was used up pretty fast and he began to feel the pinch. His loose living caught up with him and now he was forced to face reality. Penniless and hungry, in a time of famine, he must search now for work, any kind of work.

Why is it that when we're out of money, it seems everybody we know is too? Why does it seem that when our possessions are all gone, so are our friends?

So "he went and joined himself to one of the citizens of that country, who sent him into his fields to feed swine." *He sent him!* He wasn't asked; *he was sent!* It was a job lower than the bottom rung of the ladder in Jewish life: feeding and caring for pigs. This was the most loathsome work a Jew could be given to do on the farm of a foreigner! And the prodigal was so hungry that even the pig's diet was appetizing. But he wasn't even offered corn husks.

In that moment he went through a severe identity crisis. He had looked for himself in freedom from parental restraint and in protest against the stuffy respectability of his father's household. He had looked also for his identity in the squandering of his inheritance and in breaking away from the establishment.

And now Luke tells us in one incisive phrase: *"He came to himself."* Was it like waking from a bad dream? Had he found himself? At the cost of losing all?

What did he find? He was hungry, lonely, both shamed and ashamed. Which self did he discover? Like the core of an onion when peeled away, he was stripped of everything. He discovered that if you gaze at your navel long enough, you realize that it's an umbilical tie with your past, that your existence depends on, and is linked to, others.

"When he came to himself" or as one translator puts it, "When he came to his right mind," in the next breath, he said, "I will arise and go to my father." He was empty and homesick. He had learned the hard way the first lesson in identity: *we can't know who we are until we know to whom we belong.* We are belonging creatures, relational beings. No man—no woman— is an island. Augustine in his prayer affirmed for us all, "Thou has made us for thyself, O God, and our hearts are restless 'til they find their rest in thee." What a fool he'd been!

"I will arise and go to my father." But you can't go home again. No, not in the same mood you left. So he rehearsed his speech. "Father, I have sinned against heaven and before you; I am no longer worthy to be called your son." The test of the sincerity of his repentance is found in his appeal: "Treat me as one of your hired servants" (v. 19). He came to himself— daring to face the facts about himself. He looked truth squarely in the face. He dared to look at himself frankly and to discover who he was: a boy perishing with hunger, a young rebel starving to death, and needlessly so, because his father had servants who were better off than he was. I will get out of here, go home, and tell my father the plain truth that I have discovered about myself. "I have sinned against heaven and before you; I am no longer worthy to be called your son."

This, brothers and sisters, is confession! He swallowed his pride. He had left home talking about his rights, what his father owed him. He returned home and instead of talking about his rights, he was begging—for work he had previously scorned.

There is another lesson the prodigal son learned in this journey away and back: something of the meaning of *freedom*. His notion of freedom when he left—"I want out!"—meant escape from discipline and restriction. He sought freedom and ended up losing freedom. "Give me," he said to his father. "I want to be free. I want to do as I please." He wanted license—not freedom! Before the story ends, we hear him beg, "Treat me as one of your hired servants!" The road he traveled seeking freedom led to slavery. He ended up falling into the worst bondage there is—being sent into the field to feed pigs.

There is no freedom without responsibility. So, in his returning, in his willingness to do the chores of the hired hands, he began to learn the other side of freedom: the power to become what one ought. This positive freedom is rooted in a self-imposed discipline. Robert Frost defined authentic freedom as "working easy in harness." It is equally true for any area of life. One is led from a false understanding of "freedom from" to a true notion of "freedom for."

Let me inject here that in the three parables of Luke the shepherd went looking for his wandering sheep; the woman swept the floor to find the lost coin; but the father did not search for his wayward boy. The first two stories tell of the *seeking* love of God; the story of the prodigal tells of the *waiting* love of God.

The son had to choose to return, to be sure, but the father was waiting and watching. "His father saw him," Luke says, "and had compassion, and ran and embraced him and kissed him." All this happened before the son had the chance to give his rehearsed speech. The father said, "Bring quickly the best robe, and put it on him; and put a ring on his hand, and shoes on his feet; and bring the fatted calf and kill it, and let us eat and make merry; for this my son was dead, and is alive again; he was lost, and is found" (Luke 15:22-24).

A classic story of a father welcoming home a wayward child. A boy was lost. A son was found. *It is a testimony of the truth of the gospel: behind all is a great heart of love and goodness.* It is a story of one who waits with eager longing for the moment when each son or daughter abandons the self-centered life to take his or her place in the family. The father waits in love and hope. The son is received and restored!

Ray Balcomb tells about a man in England who was disturbed about the problems of juvenile crime. He tried to do something about it. He bought an old, rambling house and asked the courts to assign to his custody the juveniles they couldn't seem to handle. The man took the juveniles in and tried to make them part of a family. He won a few and lost a few, but he achieved such generally startling results that criminologists and social workers all over England began to study his methods and to ask what his secret was. He said that his best results had come from practicing a "love that waits."

Some years ago on Detroit television I interviewed Keith Miller, a layman whose honest struggle in faith brought him face-to-face with God. His story has touched thousands who did not know how to pray or how to witness about Christ without embarrassment. Through him people have learned to live socially and vocationally as committed Christians as God has touched them.

In *The Taste of New Wine* Miller tells of the time in his life when everything was closing in on him and he thought he was losing his mind. There seemed to be no hope, no ultimate purpose, nothing but despair. One day when he was driving the company car through the piney woods of East Texas, he pulled off the road and stopped.

> Now there was no tomorrow in my situation. I was like a man on a great gray treadmill going no place, in a world that was made up of black, black clouds all around me.
> As I sat there I began to weep like a little boy. . . . I looked up toward the sky. There was nothing I wanted to do with my life. And I said, "God, if there's anything you want in this stinking soul, take it"[2]

As in the experience of the prodigal, God was able to touch Keith in his moment of truth that day in a profoundly new and personal way.

There wasn't any ringing of bells or flashing of lights or visions; but it was a deep intuitive realization of what it is God wants from a man, which I had never known before. . . . I realized then that God does not want a man's money, nor does He primarily want his time. . . . He wants your *will;* and if you give Him your will, He'll begin to show you life as you've never seen it before.[3]

This realization was like being "born again." With that experience of personal contact with his heavenly Father, Keith Miller came in touch with himself and with the very meaning of life.

God was waiting for this moment in Keith's life. Unlike the prodigal who had wasted his substance in riotous living, Keith had been what the church considers a model Christian. He cared for his parents emotionally and spiritually. At the time he was happily married. His search for a vital meaningful faith had led him to Divinity School. His honesty, integrity, and good conscience, however, led him out of the theological setting and back to the marketplace. He wore a mask of confidence before the world, but God knew his heart. And a loving God was waiting.

The church today is filled with people who outwardly reflect peace and contentment but whose hearts cry out for someone to love them just as they are—lost, confused, frustrated, sometimes frightened, guilty, and often unable to communicate even with their families. We need a faith that includes biblical truths and doctrine. Even more, we need a faith that links us to a personal fellowship with a loving Father who is waiting for us to return home!

In the Book of Isaiah is a famous and stirring line. The prophet describes people who "shall renew their strength . . . mount up with wings as eagles . . . run, and not be weary . . . walk, and not faint."

Who are these extraordinarily fortunate and gifted people?

"They that wait upon the Lord" (Isa. 40:31 KJV).

The book *Laughing into Glory,* by H. M. Engleson, is

an autobiography of a Methodist preacher on his first charge. He tells of a saintly woman, Mother Morgan, who kept a blue lamp burning in her window for thirty years to welcome her vagabond son who had run away. Was she optimistic? Perhaps so. Was she a fool? Some probably said she was. Was she a woman of faith? Faith in what? Did she have faith in the unlikely return of her son? I don't know. But she did have faith in a Christ whose way it is to wait to welcome any of this flock who return to him. This is the life of faith.

And when the son came to himself he said, "I will arise and go to my father, and . . . say to him, 'Father, I have sinned . . . ; I am no longer worthy to be called your son; treat me as one of your hired servants.' " . . . While he was yet at a distance, his father saw him and had compassion, and ran and embraced him. . . . "For this my son . . . was lost, and is found."

> Amazing grace! how sweet the sound
> That saved a wretch like me!
> I once was lost, but now am found,
> Was blind, but now I see.
> *John Newton*

"There was a rich man, who was clothed in purple and fine linen and who feasted sumptuously everyday. And at his gate lay a poor man named Lazarus, full of sores, who desired to be fed with what fell from the rich man's table; moreover the dogs came and licked his sores. The poor man died and was carried by the angels to Abraham's bosom. The rich man also died and was buried; and in Hades, being in torment, he lifted up his eyes, and saw Abraham far off and Lazarus in his bosom. And he called out, 'Father Abraham, have mercy upon me, and send Lazarus to dip the end of his finger in water and cool my tongue; for I am in anguish in this flame.' But Abraham said, 'Son, remember that you in your lifetime received your good things, and Lazarus in like manner evil things; but now he is comforted here, and you are in anguish. And besides all this, between us and you a great chasm has been fixed, in order that those who would pass from here to you may not be able, and none may cross from there to us.' And he said, 'Then I beg you, father, to send him to my father's house, for I have five brothers, so that he may warn them, lest they also come into this place of torment.' But Abraham said, 'They have Moses and the prophets; let them hear them.' And he said, 'No, Father Abraham; but if some one goes to them from the dead, they will repent.' He said to him, 'If they do not hear Moses and the prophets, neither will they be convinced if some one should rise from the dead' "* **(Luke 16:19-31).**

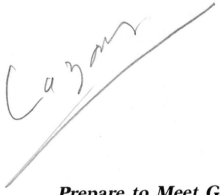

Prepare to Meet God

On an exit ramp leading from Detroit's Chrysler Freeway to Tiger Stadium, there is a sign which exhorts the passersby, "Prepare to Meet God." Obviously it was meant to remind us that for each of us life on this earth will one day end, and we should begin now thinking and living in such a way that when the moment arrives we are prepared to meet God. You have seen these signs along the roadways, on bumper stickers, and occasionally on national television when the cameras scan a crowded stadium at some sporting event.

While the exhortation is not to be scorned or ignored, it prompts me to suggest that people might better be counseled to prepare to meet God in the next person one meets or the next event in one's life instead of waiting for some final moment of death and judgement.

Luke's Gospel alone tells the story of a man who daily had the opportunity to prepare to meet God. It is the story of the rich man and the poor man; the story of Dives and Lazarus. It is a story which, in addition, paints a picture of the mysterious landscape we call heaven and hell. We're told how a rich man who had it so good in this life, ends up in hell and how a poor man, who received little but misery in life, is ultimately comforted. In the afterlife there is a remarkable reversal of their conditions. The poor man is enriched; the rich man is impoverished.

This parable is a one-act drama with three scenes.

The opening scene is set in ancient Palestine and the cast of characters pantomime the story. "There was a rich man," Luke says. Dives, he is called, is feasting and fattening his body everyday. He not only lives sumptuously but he possesses a magnificent wardrobe. He is richly clothed and richly housed. Bear in mind that Jesus in telling this parable, does not say, nor even infer, that the rich man is necessarily a bad man.

Dives is no drunkard, no gambler spending the rent money on the horses. He is neither a dope addict nor a man with a long criminal record. On the contrary, he is obviously one of the leading citizens of the town. He is wealthy, which in itself may be a mark of some distinction in our world, especially since, in this case, there is no history that he came by his money dishonestly. He is no skinflint. A miser does not live in luxury as Dives lived. He has not only wealth, but taste; and what more do we ask of a man of means but culture.

His clothes are custom-made by the finest fashion tailor in town and his table is set as only by a man with his discerning palate. He is well-dressed, well-fed, well-housed, and well-heeled. The rich man has everything: wealth, taste, position, and elegance. Many Americans today are willing to spend their lives and mortgage their futures to duplicate his life-style.

A certain beggar appears in this tableau and his condition is in ghastly contrast to this man of wealth. Every day he is dropped off at the gate of the rich man's palatial home. His name is Lazarus, which means "God is my helper." As a matter of fact, apart from God, the man appears to be completely ignored. He is emaciated by hunger and lives on the garbage from the rich man's table. He craves the scraps that fall from the rich man's table. He is prostrated by illness, covered with ulcerated sores, and so helpless that he cannot keep the street dogs from licking his sores.

Surely, as Lazarus lay by the gate of the rich man's

porch, Dives must have looked at him or passed him numerous times a day. Like many of us who look at people, yet do not see them, Dives never *saw* Lazarus. He carefully insulated himself from the beggar. At least he felt no compassion, no genuine feeling for this man in rags who was covered with sores.

His failure is absurdly simple and frighteningly ordinary. He never recognized Lazarus as anyone other than a beggar. He never wondered about Lazarus as Lazarus—a person with feelings and ambitions and longings. The beggar was just an old man with empty dreams and frustrated ambitions, just another of life's derelicts—sick, old, poor, forgotten. Lazarus was not Lazarus, a person with a name; Lazarus was just the beggar at the gate.

Whatever images you may recall from television or news magazines about the hunger and widespread poverty of Ethiopia or Calcutta and the bloated or emaciated victims of starvation, here you have a similar picture. Do you see the contrast: the rich man has everything; the poor man has nothing.

The curtain comes down on the first scene.

Scene two takes place in the next world. What happens in this second scene will happen in time to each of us. Lazarus dies. There is no mention of a funeral or a burial for the beggar, only that angels bear him to heaven, to glory, to Abraham's bosom. Dives also dies and is buried, probably with elaborate ritual and floral displays.

Helmut Thielicke, in his graphic sermon on this parable, depicts the rich man looking at his own funeral. He suggests the rich man had imagined during his life what a splendid affair his own funeral would be. All the charities he had funded would turn out in mass, all the poor he had helped through the United Way would bewail his dying, and the best preacher in town would preach him into heaven.

However, Thielicke says, "Now he actually sees his

own funeral." He sees it, not from glory, but from torment, and his whole understanding of reality is suddenly altered. It is a magnificent funeral, to be sure, but it is "oppressively different from the way it appeared to his coquettish fantasy."

In his wretched states:

> He hears a shovelful of earth come thumping down on his coffin and one of his best cronies saying, "He lived life for its own sake." And he wants to interject (though nobody hears him): "I failed to live; I am in anguish in this flame."
>
> Then the second shovelful falls and again the clods of earth come thudding down on his mahogany casket. "He loved the poor in the city," says another voice. And the rich man wants to shriek, "Oh, if you only suspected what the truth is; I am in anguish in this flame."
>
> Then the minister, the popular and beloved "abbé" of society, casts the third shovelful: "He was so religious. He donated bells, windows and a seven-branched candlestick. Peace be to his ashes." And again the clods of earth come rumbling down on his coffin. Or is it the rumbling of the crater of hell? "I am in anguish in this flame."[1]

The silence on our stage is suddenly shattered by the painfully hopeless dialogue being shouted across that chasm between torment and consolation: "And [Dives] called out, 'Father Abraham, have mercy upon me, and send Lazarus to dip the end of his finger in water and cool my tongue; for I am in anguish in this flame.' But Abraham said, 'Son, remember that you in your lifetime received your good things, and Lazarus, in like manner, evil things; but now he is comforted here, and you are in anguish' " (Luke 16:24-25).

As Lazarus on earth craved a scrap of bread now Dives in the next world craves a drop of water.

Why is he in torment? What sin did he commit? Never did the rich man order the police or his servants to remove the poor man from his gate. He never stopped his household from taking the bread crumbs to the beggar. There is no indication that he verbally or physically mistreated Lazarus. Was he ever deliberately cruel to him?

No, Dives was guilty of none of these things. *His sin was that he never noticed Lazarus.* The rich man is condemned to Hades, not because of other sins or because being rich is in itself a sin, but because he chose to neglect a poor outcast, called Lazarus, begging at his gate. No doubt the town was full of beggars, just as the town was full of stray dogs. One simply had to learn to live with them. As someone once put it, "It was not what Dives *did* that got him into torment; it was what he *did not do* that sent him to hell."

And what about Lazarus?

The poor man, his sorrows on earth ended, is carried "by the angels to Abraham's bosom" or to a place by the side of Abraham in that part of the hereafter that is called Paradise. He is feasting with the patriarchs at a celestial banquet. At this point Lazarus becomes a minor actor in the drama.

Let us be reminded, though, that this is a parable and that our Lord spoke in word pictures and symbols. These symbols are signs, not literal facts. (I am not saying that Jesus did not believe in a hereafter but he gave no instruction about that land beyond death. And, as George Buttrick has so incisively remarked, "We must be faithful to our ignorance and to His reticence."[2] There are, however, piercing realities behind the symbols of this parable: recognition, self-consciousness, memory, and moral concern.

Although in torment, Dives' vision stretches across eternity and recognizes Lazarus in Paradise. There is a yawning chasm between them, and no one can cross from one side to the other. Lazarus cannot cross it. Dives cannot cross it. The great gulf separates—now and forever. The acceptable time, the *kairos,* is past and gone.

The curtain falls on scene two.

Sometime later the rich man's memory and moral concern prompts him to ask Abraham to send Lazarus back to earth. Surely, if the chasm between heaven and hell cannot be bridged, then perhaps Lazarus can go back to earth and warn the rich man's five brothers before it is too late. In other words, he wants to warn them that their choices in the world will have dire consequences in the life to come. "But Abraham said, 'They have Moses and the prophets [they have Holy Scripture] let them hear them.' "

He does not deny that they could avoid his fate by living according to their Scriptures, but he tacitly admits that they won't. They will go on, living as they did when Dives was alive, without the slightest notion that their eternal destiny hangs in the balance. This is the sting in the parable of Lazarus and Dives. The rich man is thinking that all his five brothers need is some stupendous miracle that will open their eyes, convince them to repent, and change the direction of their lives. If this poor beggar, whom they surely knew, and doubtless saw when he died, were to return to earth with a personal message from their dead brother, it would turn the trick. But Abraham yields not to the plea: "If they do not hear Moses and the prophets, neither will they be convinced if some one should rise from the dead."

The curtain falls on scene three!

And there is no curtain call!

One further observation before we leave the story: notice that even at the end of the parable Dives is blind to his own blindness. There is no remorse, no contrition. He is concerned about himself only, his family, the tight little island of his world. What happened to him was apparently not of his own doing, but rather an unkind trick of fate. "Go tell my brothers, lest they also come to this place of torment. Someone should warn them!" Even in torment Dives tries to justify himself and his life. He was still "blind to his blindness" and so the gulf was impassable, even for God!

Most Christians sense this parable points up a lesson in practical Christianity about those who are rich and those who are poor. Some have gone so far as to believe it is a condemnation of riches and exaltation of poverty. It appears to be a story Jesus told of a great squaring of accounts in the next world. I have heard this parable preached with the supposed truth of God balancing our accounts in the hereafter. In other words, the rich get theirs on earth and those who got the short end of the stick on earth get theirs in heaven.

The key to the parable, as far as I am concerned, is not in our identifying with the rich man or the poor man. It is only as one identifies oneself with the five brothers and understands rightly the teaching of the Old and New Testaments that one finds the key to unlock the central mystery of this parable.

Lazarus and Dives are dead. The five brothers are still alive on earth. They will die, as shall we, for we share a common mortality. The brothers have Moses and the prophets who have spoken of the rewards and punishments in the next world. Those who will not listen to the eternal truth will not change their hearts by any sign. People are not redeemed by signs. The plain truth is we are inheritors of God's Word. If that does not persuade us to follow Christ on the road of life, nothing will. Redeemed, we see with the eyes of the heart: sorrow to be comforted, need to be supplied, pain to be relieved, people to be loved as children of God. If we are unmoved and do nothing about the poverty, hunger, and pain about us, we are likewise guilty. Dives did nothing wrong. The tragedy is, he did nothing!

Every day you and I stand at some crossroad. We are to be prepared to meet God at that crossroad. We need not look for the heavens to open or listen for audible voices. God is not to be expected to perform a miracle. Nor do we need some encounter with the occult to bring us to our knees. As someone has said, "God is no shock therapist who works upon our nerves; he loves you as his child and it's your heart he wants."

Let us take a look at ourselves, you and me, in our world. Many of us, far too many, do not see the poor at our gates. If we do see them, we don't recognize them as persons. They are the invisible poor. They are so invisible that many people simply refuse to believe that one-fifth of all the families living in America are poor.

One reason many of us do not see them is that they're not at our door. They are off the main thoroughfares. They live down the side alleys or up the country roads that you and I never travel. They are crowded together on the other side of the tracks, in those sections of the city that we have no occasion to visit or which we avoid. There are pockets of poverty in your town or city or country that you may have never seen.

It's difficult for us to be convinced that there is within our society a subculture in which the American dream is dying because this subculture has been so effectively concealed. We cannot bring ourselves to believe that there are homes near us where when it rains at night everyone gets up to move the beds away from the leaking roofs. There are homes with no electricity, where discarded refrigerators are valued for keeping food safe from rats, where regularly in the last week of the month whole families live on bread and hardly anything else, where children in winter sleep in burlap bags on icy floors. This is the other America, that part of American life we have so long overlooked as if it did not exist—poverty in the midst of plenty.

Like Dives, we do not want to be put into an uncomfortable position. Don't we live rather decent lives along with a lot of rather decent people? Do we differ very much from the accepted pattern of life around us? Aren't we pleasant, sociable, polite, kind, even to beggars and stray dogs?

After all, we're generous with our food baskets for the poor at Thanksgiving and Christmas. Occasionally, we give a handout to a beggar on the city street. We have mental institutions and halfway houses for the retarded. Through our taxes we take care of the prisoners behind bars. These people, after all, are not persons, really. They are only social problems.

As for the unemployed, I'm fortunate not to be counted in their number and, if they really wanted a job, they could find one. I'm not going to feel sorry for them.

Is this what you've been thinking? In our easy conscience we coast along with these situations as they are. Or do we wait until the problem becomes social dynamite before we move into action?

The church is called to speak forcefully about the downright immorality of the situation. The paradox of poverty in the midst of plenty should make us exceedingly uncomfortable. Instead, many of us choose to believe that "poor people are lazy. They could make it, too, if they'd go to work." But is that true?

Social scientists and recent studies of hard core poverty have found that a majority of the chronically poor in America began life in a strait jacket of handicaps from which most of them can never escape without help. It is easy for us who have "made it" to encourage others to pull themselves up by their own bootstraps; but some people have no bootstraps. It is easy for us to stand before our altars of abundance and sing the Doxology while millions of children in America exist on inadequate diets—so lacking in basic nutrients that minds and bodies are hopelessly stunted before they reach school age.

Men and women of Christian conscience may honestly differ over the nuclear arms race or other national political and economic issues, but hunger and poverty are clear-cut issues. Compassionate caring is the cornerstone of Christian commitment. Capitalism today is on trial and the issue is: Can capitalism be truly compassionate?

One Sunday morning a few minutes before worship a

layman knocked on my study door at Metropolitan Church. He apologized for the intrusion at that moment and handed me an envelope saying, "Read this after church."

I opened the envelope later and this was the message:

In the midst of this terrible recession which has hit Detroit large numbers of people are discouraged, out of work, hungry, and cold. Many are surely finding their way to our church. During our morning devotions today, Dorothy and I decided that no one in real need should be turned away. We don't want our pastor to be unable to help meet their needs whether it be food, fuel, medicine, or whatever. Take the proceeds from the enclosed and put it to work among the needy of Detroit. We wouldn't want to make it to the Pearly Gates and have St. Peter turn us away because we had plenty and enough to spare while others were starving or freezing to death.

On the substantial gift enclosed were the words: "To the glory of God and for the work of Jesus Christ through his Church." It was signed: Stanley S. Kresge. Stan has been for me a symbol of redeemed capitalism.

Paul said to the church at Thessalonica, "We were ready to share with you not only the gospel of God but also our own selves" (I Thess. 2:8). Paul's plea to the twentieth-century Christian is the same as to the first-century church: "Be concerned! For if you get to the place where you don't care, then God have mercy."

And remember, the only story our Lord ever told of a person going to hell was about a rich man who ignored a beggar's need and allowed him to die on his own front doorstep.

One day the Pharisees asked Jesus, "When will the Kingdom of God begin?" Jesus replied, "The Kingdom of God isn't ushered in with visible signs. You won't be able to say, 'It has begun here in this place or there in that part of the country.' For the Kingdom of God is within you" **(Luke 17:20-21 TLB).**

Jesus Is Coming—Soon?

There is an ancient tale told about how God hid the true meaning of life.

It is said that before God created human beings he discussed with his angels the subject of where he could hide the meaning of life. He wanted the secret to be found only after a great deal of trouble and search.

One of the angels suggested that the secret should rest at the bottom of the sea. Another recommended it be placed in the bowels of the earth, and a third suggested the secret be hidden on the highest mountain summit. A fourth angel objected because he thought that humans would eventually search out all of these places. Finally, God understood and said, "The only place that human beings will never dream of looking for the secret of life is in the hardest place for them to see—*within themselves.*"

During this season of Lent, when the search for meaning is so emphasized in our spiritual lives both as Christians and as human beings, we have to understand that the real answers do not lie in our mountaintop experiences or in the depths of depression but in our hearts. It is in the heart and soul of people that the kingdom of God finds its true home. Jesus intuitively understood this.

As a Jew steeped in the Word of his people he knew the promise that one day God would intervene to vindicate the right and to save his oppressed children. The kingdom of God—or the reign of God—would become a living and present reality in the hearts of his people.

The religious leaders of Jesus' day came to him and asked a question, "When is the kingdom of God coming?" Jesus answered, "The kingdom of God does not come with signs that you can watch for; nor will they say, 'Look here!' or 'Look there!'—the kingdom of God is *within* you."

There were those, to be sure, who found Jesus' response baffling just as there are those today who find it unsettling.

This little exchange between Jesus and the Pharisees has occasioned many different interpretations.

Jesus knew that his people—the Jews—had long searched the Scriptures, prayed, and waited for the coming of the Messiah in the fulfillment of prophecy. Looking toward the Messianic Age was a consolation to all believers in every critical time. It was the hope that motivated the righteous to hold onto the things of God despite the terrible events happening around them.

Today hearts are yearning for a similar consolation as the darkness deepens in political, educational, moral, and spiritual arenas. The message "comfort ye, comfort ye my people" is still apt.

What did Jesus do when he responded to the Pharisees question regarding the coming of the kingdom of God? He confounded them by not giving a sign. Instead he says, "The kingdom of God is *within* you." Is he saying there is utter futility in signs? Look inside yourself? What does he mean?

Many biblical scholars believe he meant two things.

William Barclay says Jesus meant the kingdom of God works within the hearts of people.[1] God's rule is, here and now, a spiritual reality operative in our hearts. The kingdom of God is an inward and spiritual reality rather than an outward and visible sign. The kingdom, or the rule of God, is not a revolution in the world. Instead, it is a revolutionary change evident in the lives of persons.

The other possibility is that Jesus himself embodied the kingdom.[2] It (he) is already present—"in the midst of you"—and you do not recognize him. In other words the kingdom of God is "among you" now, and you take no time to observe its (his) presence.

The evidence seems clear that even Jesus knew the kingdom would not come by human means but by an act of God and, indeed, was now present.

Is there a message for us in this understanding?

Along country roads and city freeways we read the sign: "Jesus is coming soon." Premillennial stirrings will increasingly puzzle Christians during the final decade of this century. How might a follower of Christ interpret and respond to Jesus' teaching that the kingdom of God is within you?

Paul S. Scherer has said there are three dimensions to eschatology in the New Testament: Jesus has come, Jesus is coming, Jesus will come. What does this mean?

JESUS HAS COME

One tragedy in the excessive emphasis on the Second Coming is that one misses the opportunity and joy of responding to and serving a Savior who has *already* come! Even now he is with us. God appeared decisively in his Son!

The gospel is good news! *God has not come—and gone!* He is with us in Christ. Emmanuel—God himself—is with us. We fear not because the Savior has come. His name is Jesus and the Good News is: he is still saving his people from their sins. This is a reality that many today miss. God did not create his world and then abandon it. He is with us in all his grace and glory. Without this good and gracious God there would be no hope for our world.

Another tragedy in our obsession with the Second Coming is in the signal we often send to those who know little or nothing of the Savior *already* in our midst. A

48

hopelessly blind world is ceaselessly searching for a god who is no God at all. Many search for one who will be and do what they want him to be and do—a sort of universal bellhop.

There is an old story about a young woman who jilted her boyfriend because he was poor. Unexpectedly one day, he received a letter from her pleading for reconciliation and concluding with the words: "I love you very much." Beneath her signature, however, was penned a telling post script "Congratulations on the $50,000 you just inherited from your grandfather!"

Many persons do not really want what God has to give. In fact, they don't want to know him as he is. They just want to get from him what they want. Their understanding of God parallels a child's understanding of Santa Claus.

Christians, therefore, need to demonstrate that in their lives something has already been experienced of the kingdom of God. We are to bear witness to the world that the old order of things has passed away and the new order has already begun.

Let's take a look at that new order in the common thread woven through the tapestry of the New Testament.

We are in the company of John the Baptizer who announced that the kingdom of God draws near.

We are with Jesus at the beginning of his ministry when he declared, "The time is fulfilled, and the kingdom is at hand; repent, and believe in the gospel" (Mark 1:15).

We hear him tell the Pharisees, "Behold the kingdom of God is in the midst of you."

We listen to the apostles who saw the risen Christ, witnessed his ascension, and were visited by the Holy Spirit on the day of Pentecost. Peter stood up on that day and declared: "Let all the house of Israel know assuredly that God has made him both Lord and Christ, this Jesus whom you crucified."

Finally, we are in the company of Paul, who said, "If any one is in Christ, he is a new creation; the old has passed away, behold, the new has come" (II Cor. 5:17).

Jesus has *already* come? The old order of things has *already* ended? Are we sure? How can we believe this in today's world?

What has ended?

The dominance of evil has ended! That is a strange thing to say with evil so obviously present in our contemporary life. But the Christians in the New Testament knew very well that evil had been overcome. Their struggle against evil, in fact, was probably no more intense than ours, for they, too, were surrounded by a pagan culture that was cruel, superstitious, arrogant, powerful, and hostile.

Evil was all around them and it was bent on destroying, by persecution, the fledgling church that had sprung up in the midst of it. These Christians knew that evil was present and powerful, yet they also declared that it was overcome! Its power had been dealt a mortal blow.

The early church also knew the war with evil would be an ongoing struggle as long as history remained history. With the entry of Christ into that struggle the victory of God was assured. In aligning our lives with Christ, we share in his victory. This is partly what these early Christians meant when they proclaimed, "Jesus Christ is Lord!" Their word of faith to us: "The victory is his and his victory is ours! The power of sin, evil, and death has been broken! Evil has lost its grip!" To the outsider this seemed a wild and arrogant thing to say. Today to some it may still appear to be a presumptuous thing to say.

Are we still justified in saying this when we read the newspaper or watch daily life unfold in all its ugliness across the world? The believer lives with the conviction that evil will not have the final word. Christians know evil is not omnipotent because they know Jesus Christ is their Savior.

Christians know they remain sinners as long as they live, but they also know sin does not hold them in its grip because their allegiance has been given to Christ. Faith in Christ and commitment to him, when it is real, serious and sincere, brings one into contact with a new order: the kingdom of God! Jesus has already come and reigns!

JESUS IS COMING

Second, the Christian knows Jesus is coming.

We live in the *knowledge* that Jesus *has* come and with an *assurance* that he *is* coming. The kingdom of God entered our world in Jesus and Jesus taught: "The kingdom is within." He daily confronts men and women with his beckoning call, "Follow me."

The overriding fact of our age is change. One consequence of rapid change is a subtle and pervasive feeling of uneasiness. In a world of uncertainty the church needs to proclaim anew that Jesus is coming. In an age when what is new today may be obsolete next year, it is reassuring to know Jesus is the same yesterday, today, and forever. The Christian is called to be ever vigilant and alert to his coming and to give a witness of the presence of an unchanging Christ in this unstable world.

What then, is wrong with our witness? All too often we have a million things distracting us, and we don't want to be bothered having to respond to religious jargon! That's the trouble with us—a million things to do! We have eyes for little else and whatever *need* we see turns into a "thing" to be "handled." While our world is filled with *persons in need*, we materialistic people miss the meaning of life and the opportunities of a lifetime. We have been reminded that, as Christians, we are to love people and use things. Too many of us are prone to the opposite: we use people and love things.

This is a complex religious age. The simplicity of Jesus is rarely found among us. Instead, our programs, activities, methods, and organizations occupy our time and attention, though seldom do thy satisfy the longings of our heart. United Methodist Bishop Richard Wilke, in an interview, has spoken to his denomination's present condition: "Our methodology approaches madness, our organizational genius consumes our most sophisticated talent. Our structure has become an end in itself, not a means of saving the world." Bishop Wilke goes on:

> I became intensely aware of this myopia when I was a pastor. The evangelism committee met, but did not make any calls. The social concerns commission gathered, but did not read from the Bible. The Council on Ministries assembled to hear reports from the committees, but took little action. The Administrative Board sat in session to approve the budget, but no one was saved. We went home tired, thinking we had done our church work.[3]

The inner-life experience is shallow. Our worship is routine and hollow. Our servile imitation of the world marks our promotional methods and testifies that we know the ways of the world better than we understand the ways of God. We know God imperfectly and the peace of God scarcely at all. The encrusted habit of self-interest and greed grips us. We are numb to goodness, deaf to truth, and blind to beauty, and we miss friendships, good times, and happiness—and, many even miss Jesus!

One basic cause of frustration has been the eclipse of faith in the Western world. Too many are possessed by a great fear rather than a great faith. Many voices call us; many ways beckon us. Let the voice of the Master remind us, "What shall it profit a man, if he shall gain the whole world, and lose his own soul?" (Mark 8:36 KJV).

How, then, do we make our witness?

Truly convinced that God has shown his love in the life, death, and resurrection of Christ, we show gratitude by loving our neighbors as we do ourselves. What we do to the least of his children, we do unto him. We begin to fulfill our Christian obligation by promoting love and justice.

God has placed us in this world to witness and to work. We don't retreat from such work. We accept this task despite its uncertainty and confusion and seek to infuse it with the reconciling love of God. This work in the world is God's call for us to use the talent he has given us. We do not wring our hands in despair. We do not abandon life in the world anymore than God has abandoned his creation. We accept the risk involved.

If our tendency is to despair at the magnitude of our problems, let us recall past victories through which God's church has triumphed. The witness of the church over twenty centuries is glorious and reassuring.

Can we affirm a faith that proclaims Jesus is coming? Can we live lives worthy of him who is present— daily—within? Let the evidence be demonstrated through the work of the Spirit manifested within the church and among the people of God. Jesus is actively coming among his followers, still!

For our faith lies not in the things of this world nor even in those things hoped for in the next. Our faith is in the God who created us to live both in this world and in the next. In this trust and faith, the Christian lives ever alert because Jesus is coming! at every turn.

JESUS WILL COME AGAIN

If as Christians, we know Jesus has come and Jesus is coming, there is still the cherished belief that Jesus will come again to consummate the Kingdom. The roadway sign "Jesus is coming soon," which we laugh at or ignore, can be a reminder to the contemporary church

53

of the faith of our early church fathers and mothers.

Among scholars the technical term for this return is Parousia[4]—from the Greek word meaning coming or presence. The imminent return of Jesus was a dominating force in the thinking of the early Christians. Jesus would come again within their lifetime.

The early church was an eschatological community eagerly awaiting the return of its Lord. "Remember this. There are some here who will not die until they have seen the Kingdom of God come with power" (Mark 9:11 GNB). "Remember this! All these things will happen before the people now living have all died" (Mark 13:30 GNB).

The years rolled on. Jerusalem fell without the coming of the end.

Luke, I believe, eliminated the idea of imminent expectation and replaced it with the concept of an end-time—remote in history. Today's church, rather than waiting on tiptoe for the Parousia to occur at any moment, should concentrate on continuing her witness in the world in the midst of godless surroundings and in the midst of persecution.

Paul thought he had only his lifetime to announce to the world the arrival of the reign of God and to invite people to accept or reject it. In several of his early letters, Paul considered it quite unlikely that anyone would die before the early return of Jesus.

The first-century church believed with deep conviction that the Second Coming was near, but that simply did not come to pass. The first generation gave way to the second and the second generation gave way to the third. It became increasingly clear that the church's expectation of the imminent return of Christ was not to be met.

How then does one interpret the New Testament teachings about the end-time in light of such compelling expectations demonstrated by the early Christians?

We have lost this sense of urgency. We must regain it not because the time is short, but because of the importance of the task . . . to mediate God to man. The only right time to rescue people from their sins and the consequence of their sins is now, immediately.[5]

There is no doubt that the Gospel writers, Paul, and the early church believed the end was near. There are numerous references—"the time is near," "I am coming soon." They were convinced that they would witness the return of Christ. That they were proved to be wrong does not invalidate the message. It simply illustrates that the wisdom of Jesus in this matter is more dependable. At the end of the "little apocalypse" in Mark 13 Jesus says, "But of that day or that hour no one knows, not even the angels in heaven, nor the Son, but only the Father" (v. 13). As for the end of the world and the Second Coming it is for God to know, not us.

We need to go beyond the literal to the symbolic. We have to move away from the concentration on every little brush stroke to where we can see the entire canvas. As Charles Layman has said, "It is the moral and spiritual meaning that is central and not the package in which it is wrapped."

We have an invincible faith at the heart of our religion. The fundamentalist may sing, "This world is not my home, I'm just passing through," but God has made this world and wants us to be at home in it.

Yet, it is true we live not in one world but in two, and it is the spiritual not the physical that endures. "For we know that, if our earthly house of this tabernacle were dissolved, we have a building of God, a house not made with hands, eternal in the heavens" (II Cor. 5:1 KJV).

As Augustine, the aged Bishop of Hippo, lay dying in the year 430, a ship was seen approaching the North African port where he lived. There was something ominous about its arrival. What news did it bring? The whole city ran out to meet it. Soon a member of the bishop's household came running into the bishop's

55

bedroom and excitedly exclaimed, "Rome has been invaded by the Goths! They have sacked the city! Rome, the eternal city, is destroyed." Calmly, and with vision that belonged perhaps only to the dying, the old saint replied, "Rome may be destroyed but the City of God remains."

The world as we know it may someday be destroyed. This is a grim possibility. But, Christians, rejoice! Jesus has come! Jesus is coming! And . . . Jesus will come again!

> The body they may kill;
> God's truth abideth still;
> His kingdom is forever.

And he came out, and went, as was his custom, to the Mount of Olives; and the disciples followed him. And when he came to the place he said to them, "Pray that you may not enter into temptation." And he withdrew from them about a stone's throw, and knelt down and prayed, "Father, if thou art willing, remove this cup from me; nevertheless not my will, but thine, be done." And when he rose from prayer, he came to the disciples and found them sleeping for sorrow, and he said to them, "Why do you sleep? Rise and pray that you may not enter into temptation" **(Luke 22:39-46)**.

Prayer Changes Things?

The story is told in Michigan of a woman who purchased at a craft fair a piece of needlework that contained as part of the design the words, "Prayer Changes Things." Proud of her choice, she took it home and hung it above the fireplace in the family room. Several days later she noticed that it was missing and, by questioning her husband, found that he was the one who had taken it down. She asked him if it disturbed him because he did not believe in the power of prayer. He responded by saying, "No, it's not that. I believe in prayer. In fact, I believe that it changes things. I just don't happen to like change and so I took it down!"

From the days of my boyhood, I have seen signs like that piece of handiwork and heard people repeat that pseudo-religious adage: "Prayer changes things." Yet, when I consult the New Testament and read Jesus' response to the disciples' request to "teach us to pray," I find that the prayer he taught them says nothing about changing things. It's doubtful whether prayer changes *things*. Jesus prayed in Gethsemane but it didn't change things for the Master. Three times Paul prayed for *his* "thorn in the flesh" to be removed and three times his prayer didn't change his condition. Down through the ages, history is replete with the great spirits and the common folk who have found that prayer does not change things. The effect of prayer on the material facts of environment and existence is secondary; its primary effect is to change *people.*

Seeing Jesus at prayer profoundly moved his disciples, who had been feeling powerless and ineffective. On that occasion with one voice, they asked Jesus, "Lord, teach us to pray." He answered their request by voicing the perfect prayer.

Listen again to Jesus' words:

"When ye pray, say":

> Our Father, who art in heaven, hallowed be thy name. Thy kingdom come, thy will be done on earth as it is in heaven. Give us this day our daily bread. And forgive us our trespasses, as we forgive those who trespass against us. And lead us not into temptation, but deliver us from evil. For thine is the kingdom, and the power, and the glory, forever. Amen.

Millions of Christians frequently repeat this prayer without giving thought to its perfect form and content and pass from cradle to the grave without much comprehension of its grandeur, power, and beauty.

In the Lord's Prayer, expressed desire for the fulfillment of personal needs is approved but such requests are not to come first. An attitude of reverence and humility in the presence of God precedes our passionate desires and inordinate demands. Knowing what God in his wisdom and love desires for us and responding to his will are the important lessons Jesus teaches here.

Like Jesus' other significant actions, teaching the disciples to pray takes place after he himself has prayed. Prayer was a natural and essential part of Jesus' life, not an artificial adjunct. The secret of Jesus' life was his faith in God, a faith continually manifested in prayer. He also demonstrated his faith in service, but he never substituted service for prayer. Each was linked to the other.

Jesus' fellowship with the Father extended beyond

the synagogue. To relieve life's pressures and troubles we see him retreat in solitude. When the tough times came, he sought and found strength and guidance in prayer. In the great crises he turned to God in prayer.

There is a regular rhythm in his life of prayer and work. He prayed at his baptism. The twelve apostles were chosen only after a night vigil at prayer. His countenance was changed on the Mount of Transfiguration in an act of prayer. His soul was in distress in the Garden of Gethsemane as he poured out his soul to God. In his hour of sorrow and desolation, he urged Peter, James, and John to pray. Upon the cruel cross he prayed for his murderers. His dying breath was a prayer: "Father, into thy hands I commend my spirit."

The Lord's Prayer, as Jesus prayed it, is not the pattern followed among people like you and me. Instead of coming before God "as a little child" (Mark 10:15 KJV) wanting to know his will and being prepared to follow it, we begin by asking God to grant us the desires of our heart. Or we think praying is like rubbing an Aladdin's lamp, expecting God to appear like a genie to immediately answer our every whim. It is as if we had reversed Jesus' petition, in effect saying, "Not as thou wilt, but as I will." We assume that the wisdom dwells in us.

Prayer is essential to the Christian's life. This, every serious believer recognizes. It comes more easily to some than it does to others. Often it seems like a fruitless game of hide and seek, in which we seek and God hides. All Christians pray a little, but many feel the need to pray more often; some find praying difficult. Jesus felt the need of prayer. He prayed. He taught people how to pray. He lived the kind of life that we in the depths of our being would like to live. He could not live without communing with God. Neither can we.

According to Jesus there is no such thing as unanswered prayer. "Everyone who asks receives" (Luke 11:10).

Harry Emerson Fosdick in *The Meaning of Prayer*, tells us that "God always answers true prayer in one of two ways. . . . For either he changes the circumstances or he supplies sufficient power to overcome them; he answers either the petition or the man."[1]

Adoniram Judson, the famed missionary, testified: "I never prayed sincerely and earnestly for anything, but it came; at some time—no matter at how distant a day—somehow, in some shape . . . probably the last I should have devised—it came." Glimpse his life for a moment. Judson prayed for entrance into India and instead was compelled to go to Burma. He prayed for his wife's life and buried both her and his two children. He prayed for release from the King of Ava's prison, but he was compelled to remain for months, chained and miserable. Scores of Judson's *petitions* went without an affirmative answer. But *Judson* was always answered. He was upheld, guided, reinforced. Unforeseen doors opened through the very trials he sought to avoid. And the deep desires of his life were accomplished not *in* his way but *beyond* his way.

Prayer changes things? No, prayer changes people and people change things. Through prayer God releases his power within us. Pearl Buck recalled what happened in the life of her mother, a missionary to China. On one occasion her mother was alone with her children. The maid came with the warning that bandits were coming to kill the missionary family. Her mother went to God in prayer and said, "If it be thy will, save us, but in any case, help me not to be afraid." For a long time she knelt pondering what she would do. When she rose from her knees, she had a plan of action in her mind that she valiantly carried out and that saved them all.

Pearl Buck's mother might have prayed, "God, you know this catastrophe that is about to befall us. Lord, I turn it over to you to handle. Amen." Instead she turned to God asking help to quiet the panic in the soul, to release his power in her life, and to give direction to creative action. Without prayer she would not have been equal to the situation. Prayer enabled her to become the channel through which God's creative action and divine power flowed to transform the situation from impending disaster to triumph.

Yet, God will not do for us what we can—and ought—to do for ourselves. One does not turn to prayer as the easy way out of trouble. William Barclay reminds us:

> Prayer is not an easy way out to save us from trouble. Prayer is not a means of evading our own responsibilities and of escaping our own allotted toil. We may put this in another way. No sooner have we prayed than we must set out to make our own prayers come true: prayer is the cooperation of our effort with the grace of God. It is when we make our greatest effort that God sends His greatest answer.[2]

Look at the results of Jesus' prayers. He was saved from his temptations, he was delivered from his fears, he was lifted above his anxieties. In the Garden of Gethsemane on the eve of the crucifixion, Jesus wrestled and struggled in prayer. His agony was so intense that "His sweat became like great drops of blood falling down upon the ground" (Luke 22:44).

Jesus was uncertain what God wanted him to do. He prayed, "Father, if thou art willing, remove this cup from me" (Luke 22:42*a*). But in his prayer he was able to say, "Nevertheless not my will, but thine, be done" (Luke 22:42*b*). And God did not spare him from the cross—the *thing* for which he had initially prayed. Why should we expect God to do for us what he did not do for Jesus? Instead, Jesus' commitment expressed in prayer enabled God to endow him with the strength, the confidence, the poise, the faith to meet his accusers and master a painful, cruel, shameful death. His prayer had given God the conditions under which he was able to do for his son what he is trying continually to do for us all—make us equal to life's circumstances in a Godlike spirit.

Contrary to our common assumptions, what we usually need more than anything else is not some material blessing. Nor do we need most to have our problems and difficulties magically disappear. What we need most of all is the confidence and strength and poise to face the circumstances in which we find ourselves. Fears paralyze us. Anxieties confuse us. Uncertainties cloud our judgment and inhibit our thought processes. On the other hand, prayer will almost always buttress our faith, calm our spirit, clear our mind, renew our ability to cope.

All of us will remain dwarfs in our spiritual life until there is a quickening of the life of devotion and prayer. This is a personal pilgrimage, from self to God, of which I speak.

The journey begins in a quest that leads the seeker to conversion. When we accept God's grace by faith and commit ourselves to Jesus Christ and to his way of life, the next step moves us into the Christian community by linking ourselves to Christ's body, the Church. Continuing on the way, we grow in grace and the knowledge of our Lord. Then comes an increasing awareness of how far we have fallen short of the glory of God.

Seeking a closer walk with him, we encounter struggle and inner conflict between our attraction to Jesus and our own self-interest. The debate rages inside us. Shall I give myself wholly to God or hold back? Our response in this moment determines if the conversion has been truly a spiritual awakening or merely a formal act of joining the church.

The awakening is the first of many unforgettable moments when God's nearness is felt. New life rushes in. His presence floods our soul. Prayer becomes communion—dialogue rather than monologue.

John Wesley's "heartwarming experience" was a conversion, but it was, simultaneously, an awakening.

From the time when he learned to love Jesus at his mother's knee and was taught to pray, he had been a Christian. At Aldersgate the lukewarmness of his religion changed into the flaming of a divine fire. Listen to Wesley's own description of what happened to him:

> I went unwillingly . . . while he was describing the change which God works in the heart through faith in Christ, I felt my heart strangely warmed. I felt that I did trust Christ, Christ alone for salvation, and an assurance was given me that he had taken away *my* sins, even *mine*, and saved *me* from the law of sin and death. I began to pray with all my might for those who had in a more especial manner despitefully used me and persecuted me. I then testified openly to all there what I now first felt in my heart.[3]

Mind you, Wesley's prayer life before Aldersgate could hardly be called inadequate or haphazard. Initially in his ministry, he began his day at 6 A.M. Gradually the hands of his inner time clock were moved back to 5 A.M. then permanently to 4 A.M. He began every day with prayer. John Wesley's spiritual awakening opened the clogged channels of his soul, enabling God to begin his mighty works in and through Wesley. It is an acknowledged fact that Wesley's quest brought him to that moment. The Holy Spirit touched Wesley's heart that night and he was spiritually awakened.

In the stillness of that moment—May 24, 1738, at about a quarter 'til nine in the evening—Wesley turned from self-centeredness, self-consciousness, self-will, and self-love to a real commitment and communion with his Father. He began a new adventure, a pilgrimage of prayer, and a virtual dwarf became the greatest giant of eighteenth-century England. Wesley's dark night of the soul had ended.

Each of us, at some time or other, will experience our dark night, our Gethsemane. When it comes will the source of power that comes through prayer bring us through the dark night into his marvelous light?

The strength that God gave to his Son, to Adoniram Judson, to the mother of Pearl Buck, to John Wesley, is available to you and me. We need only ask, seek, knock, pray. We will find strength we didn't have before.

Bishop Gerald Kennedy personally touched a generation of ministers through his preaching and his writing. In his autobiography he tells of the dark night of his life. Following seminary and the completion of his doctoral studies, he went to Europe. He had the world by its tail. But the secular spirit of the day, the depths of the Great Depression, the naïve confidence in science watered down the faith and Kennedy began to lose heart. He was appointed to a church, which despite his persuasive preaching and pastoral work, refused to grow. Eager for a new beginning, he took a church of smaller membership with less salary. The new church faced a heavy indebtedness, an unfinished building, and a scandal that wouldn't go away. In his own words, Kennedy confesses:

> I went through a crisis which was like a second conversion to me. I knew I could not continue as I was and if God did not do for me something which I could not do for myself, it was curtains for my chosen vocation. Then it came to me that if God had called me to the ministry, he had some responsibility for me and my work. He would see to it that people came to hear me preach and he would take my poor but honest efforts and use them for his purposes. If he wanted me to do the job, then he must be willing to give me the power to do it. All of this and more poured out of my soul in prayer.
>
> I cannot say that the end of all doubt came with this experience, nor is it true that all my living became sheer joy. But the main thing had been accomplished and it was never the same again.[4]

Kennedy found what you and I can come to know: prayer changes people and people change things.

Two others, criminals, were led out to be executed with him at a place called "The Skull." There all three were crucified—Jesus on the center cross, and the two criminals on either side.

"Father, forgive these people," Jesus said, "for they don't know what they are doing."

And the soldiers gambled for his clothing, throwing dice for each piece. The crowd watched. And the Jewish leaders laughed and scoffed. "He was so good at helping others," they said, "let's see him save himself if he is really God's Chosen One, the Messiah."

The soldiers mocked him, too, by offering him a drink—of sour wine. And they called to him, "If you are the King of the Jews, save yourself!"

A signboard was nailed to the cross above him with these words: "This is the King of the Jews" **(Luke 23:32-38 TLB)**.

The Cross and the Crap Game

Today marks the beginning of Holy Week, a time that reminds us of the suffering and death of Jesus of Nazareth.

The first Holy Week began so well. Jesus rode into Jerusalem for his final Passover week. "A triumphal entry," it is called.

The first Holy Week ended so badly. Jesus is dead, laid in a borrowed tomb, behind a sealed stone door.

Palm Sunday celebrates a very human triumph. The crowds turned out to greet him tumultuously with cries of "Hosanna" and "Son of David." The carpenter from Nazareth, the prophet from Galilee comes into his own at last. They waved palm branches, a national emblem. They hoped he would restore the national monarchy. "Blessed is he who comes in the name of the Lord! Blessed is the King of Israel!" (John 12:13 NIV).

People were cheering him and cheering for him. Jesus appeared to be on the threshold of victory. Matthew describes his entry into the Holy City this way, "When he entered Jerusalem the whole city went wild with excitement" (Matt. 21:10 NEB). John in his Gospel jots down the mumblings of the Pharisees to one another: "You see?—There's nothing one can do! The whole world is running after him" (John 12:19 Phillips). What an unintentional tribute: "The whole world is running after him!"

Today around the world Christians gather to remember that day in Jesus' life. In memory we join in their enthusiasm and shout our hosannas, "Save us now!"

In the spirit of the children's hymn, "I should like to have been with him then," let's turn back the calendar to be with him on that first Palm Sunday.

Jesus, his disciples and followers converged on the Holy City along the Jerusalem–Jericho road. Jesus knew that road. He had traveled it before. He set the story of a man robbed, beaten, left to die—and later befriended by a good Samaritan—on that road.

It was the festival of Passover. From all over the ancient known world, Jews came to Jerusalem to celebrate. It was the ambition of every Jew, wherever he lived, to observe one such Passover in Jerusalem. To this very day when Jews celebrate Passover, they say, "Next year in Jerusalem." If estimates are correct, as many as two million Jews may have been streaming into Jerusalem and the villages round about to observe this compulsory feast. The thoroughfares were jammed with all sorts of people: the devout, the religiously conservative, the curious, the camp followers, the petty thieves, the government agents. All were included among the motley crowd.

Recall in the novel *The Robe*, Marcellus, the Roman official, had a Greek servant named Demetrius who was caught up in that mob at the gates of Jerusalem on Palm Sunday. Demetrius was swept along by the jostling, pressing crowd and caught sight of Jesus advancing slowly on a donkey.

Lloyd Douglas says:

> Then Demetrius caught sight of the eyes of Jesus. Drifting about over the excited multitude, they seemed to carry a sort of wistful compassion for these helpless victims of an aggression for which they thought he had a remedy. Everyone was shouting, shouting—all except

Demetrius. His throat was so dry that he couldn't have shouted; he had no inclination to shout; he wished they would all be quiet. It wasn't the time or place for shouting. This man wasn't the sort of person one shouted at, or shouted for. As Demetrius moved away from the crowd after having faced Jesus, an uncouth Athenian, bursting with curiosity asked him:

"See him—close up?"

Demetrius nodded and turned away.

"Crazy?" persisted the Athenian, trudging alongside.

"No."

"King?"

"No," muttered Demetrius, soberly, "not a king."

"Who is he, then?" demanded the Athenian.

"I don't know," mumbled Demetrius, in a puzzled voice, "but he is something more important than a king."[1]

The question put to Demetrius sooner or later confronts us, "Who is he, then?"

Remember twenty years earlier Jesus had been in Jerusalem for Passover. Joseph and Mary, his parents, thought they had lost Jesus in a crowd like that. Jesus was twelve then. After searching for three days, they found him in the Temple "sitting among the teachers, listening to them and asking them questions, and everyone who heard him was astonished at his intelligence and at the answers he made" (Luke 2:46-47 Goodspeed). "Who is he?" the elders in the Temple surely asked! His anxious parents must have wondered when he said, "I must be about my Father's business" (Luke 2:49*b* KJV). A mystery even to his parents! It remains a puzzle two decades later on this, the first Palm Sunday.

A triumphal entry? Triumphal entries recorded in history were made after victories had been won. The Roman conqueror returning to his city, bringing captives and spoils of war, leading a long column of slaves, was welcomed with shouts and ovations.

This triumphal entry of Jesus, unlike any other in

history, came without a victory having been won. This entry could hardly be defined as triumphant. Jesus was not a conqueror like other conquerors. This was no coronation but rather an impromptu affair, with little or no preparation. He was hailed as a king. But the people saw no crown, no warrior's steed or chariot, nothing that symbolized authority or royal power.

The people saw only a Galilean peasant, dressed in the simple garb of Galilean life, seated on a beast of burden upon which a few peasants had thrown their weather-beaten cloaks. That was all. Not a king—yet more than a king?

There are few clues in this scene to prepare one for the events of the week. Hosannas, palm branches, and a donkey—that was all! Some *clues* for what would follow! Could one know that shouts of "Crucify" would follow cries of "Hosanna"? That nails would follow palm branches? That a cross would bear the man now borne by a donkey?

The incongruity of Palm Sunday is primarily due to the discrepancy between what the people expected and what Jesus intended to do. Jesus was not there as a revolutionary or as a Messiah poised to smash the Roman oppressors. Jesus had another world in mind.

Let's continue to briefly chart his movements during this tragic Holy Week.

After visiting the Temple, he retreated to Bethany for the night. The following day Jesus returned to the city. He was sick at heart over the commercialization of the Temple. In righteous anger with whip in hand, he chased the money changers out of the Temple court-yard, infuriating his enemies in the process.

Some of those enemies waited for him, seeking to entrap him. They asked, "Is it lawful to give tribute to Caesar or not?" Rome imposed taxes on the Jews to remind them of their degradation. Some Jewish leaders thought they ought not to pay taxes to a pagan government; others disagreed. The question was a perfect trap. Holding a coin in his hand, Jesus told them to "render to Caesar the things that are Caesar's, and to God the things that are God's."

The following night at supper a woman came with a vial of expensive perfume. She poured it over Jesus' head. Jesus made a cryptic remark about preparing his body for burial.

The next day Jesus left Bethany again and shared a fellowship meal in a borrowed upper room with his disciples. He revealed that one of the twelve would betray him. Not one of them pointed a finger at another or asked, "Is it he, Lord?" Instead they asked, "Is it I?" Judas slipped away, and after they had sung a psalm, they left the upper room.

In Gethsemane the solders came to arrest Jesus. Thus began a night-long ordeal of grilling and a mock trial for Jesus. Jesus Barabbas was set free by demand of the chanting mob, and Jesus of Nazareth was condemned to die.

Beaten brutally and surrounded by four Roman soldiers, Jesus was paraded through the streets dragging a cross. Because Jesus was wearied and weak from the fatigue and the scourging, Simon of Cyrene, a North African, was ordered to carry the cross.

The Romans marched the prisoners on the longest death march possible, through every street or road. The crowd followed Jesus and the condemned agitators outside the city wall to the place of crucifixion.

Crucifixion, Cicero said, was "the most cruel and horrifying death." Originated by the ancient Phoenicians and Carthaginians, crucifixion was the method used by the Roman conquerors to execute runaway slaves and revolutionaries in its occupied provinces. Jewish law prohibited such torture. Roman citizens were immune from it.

Jesus, the revolutionary, was brought to the place known as Golgotha. It was a stinking rock heap, littered with skulls and bones and crawling with vermin and reptiles.

The Roman legionnaires stripped Jesus of his clothes, shoved him flat on his back and bound his outstretched arms to the timbers. The helmeted soldiers held him down as they drove spikes through the wrists to secure the arms in place. After his feet and hands were nailed to the wood, the cross was placed in the earth.

The slow, tormenting death began. So excruciating was the agony of the crucified victims that many died screaming maniacs. Writhing in torment, slowly dying, some were known to hang there for as long as three days.

As our Lord gasped for air, his convulsive body tearing his flesh, he heard the crowd's taunts: "He saved others; let him save himself." One of the thieves crucified with him sneered, "If you are the Son of God, save yourself and us."

As if the nightmare of that terrifying scene were not enough insult and agony for one to endure, at the foot of the cross upon which Jesus was hanging, the soldiers rolled dice for the only earthly possessions of this Son of God and Son of man.

Every criminal was escorted to the place of crucifixion by four soldiers who were entitled to the clothes of the victim. The Jew wore five articles of clothing: sandals, turban, tunic, girdle, and outer robe. There were four soldiers and five articles of apparel. They threw dice and each made his choice.

The soldiers were lounging in a small circle on the ground, the leather dice cup was passed again from hand to hand. Who gets the trophy—the rumpled, bloodstained brown coat at the foot of the central cross? It was a finely woven, country homespun robe, dyed perhaps with walnut juice. It was an extraordinary seamless robe and the "King of the Jews" wouldn't be needing it anymore. To have cut it into four pieces would have made it worthless, so the soldiers rolled dice again.

Here the stake was only a robe. Here the gambling took place before the eyes of the Son of God. The soldiers gambled!

Pilate and Caiaphas had gambled too. No mere robe of a rabble-rouser for them. Pilate gambled that washing his dirty hands in a silver bowl would be the end of this troublemaker. They gambled on the proposition that the sword rules. To be rid of an agitating fanatic, you kill him and "dead men tell no tales."

Jesus gambled. Not in the sense of the soldiers, or Pilate and Caiaphas. He gambled for higher stakes. He risked everything in his faithfulness to the Father. He staked his life on God. The cross would be his final chance to prove God's love to the world. It would be the great amen of his life.

G. A. Studdert-Kennedy wrote a poem about this vivid scene. It is entitled "He Was a Gambler Too."

And, sitting down, they watched Him there,
The soldiers did;
There, while they played with dice,
He made His Sacrifice,
And died upon the Cross to rid
God's world of sin.
He was a gambler, too, my Christ,
He took His life and threw
It for a world redeemed.
And ere His agony was done,
Before the westering sun went down,
Crowning that day with its crimson crown,
He knew that He had won.[2]

On Calvary Jesus gambled for love against hate, and he won. It is this love he continually exemplified throughout his ministry. The disciples had seen his love in action as Jesus healed the sick, gave sight to the blind, and brought wholeness to men and women mired in the quicksand of sin. Zacchaeus had seen this accepting love in Jesus as he looked up at the tax collector in the sycamore tree in Jericho. A woman, whose arms had held countless men who had not loved her, had seen his forgiving love reflected in the tears that fell upon Jesus' feet before she brushed them away with her hair.

The jeering crowd surely sensed *that* love as a dying Galilean pursed his lips to pray, "Father, forgive them for they know not what they do." In his last gasping breath he cried out, "Father, into thy hands I commit my spirit," and the Roman centurion, sensing something of the divine in that moment, responded, "Surely, this man was the Son of God."

There are times in life when love appears to lose. This was one of those moments.

No scene in the Gospels portrays the calloused indifference of the world to the Son of God as does this one. Jesus was dying in agony on a hellish cross while soldiers were kneeling—not to pray—but to gamble, to satisfy their greed. They did so cruelly, untouched by the human suffering in their midst.

I am haunted by such indifference repeated too often today around our world. While hunger and homelessness, starvation and suffering afflict millions, Americans spend billions of dollars each year on gambling—more than all the money spent on education, medical care, and church support put together.

The gambling craze permeates our national life. Casinos alone take in nine billion dollars a year. Why this mania that has swept the nation? Have we lost confidence in a moral order? What has happened to the joy in ordinary work? Has a desire to "get rich quick" replaced our assurance of faith? Have we become willing to gamble it all on the spin of a wheel of fortune or a turn in a deck of cards?

The problem of "the cross and the crap game" is not confined to those who murdered Jesus or those who rolled dice for his robe. It is woven into the total fabric of our world. Its pattern and influence are universally seen.

We live with "little crucifixions" every day: dying by

violence, religious and racial discrimination, the agony of the poor. So much of the world's suffering is rooted in human failure: crimes of passion or greed, wars resulting from a lust for power and domination, crooked governments, social injustices, humanity scourged by twisted motives.

In the biblical view the taproot of it all lies in human sin, a deep-seated egocentricity, a bondage to selfishness that separates us from God, from others, and from wholeness.

A profound transaction took place on Golgotha that day. There have been various theories advanced to explain that transaction. Simply put, God revealed in Christ's death his love for us and reconciled us to our Maker. Paul Tillich said, "The cross is the central manifestation of God's participation in the suffering of the world." Paul said, "He gave himself a ransom for all." Perhaps Jesus put it best of all, "Greater love hath no man than this, that a man lay down his life for his friends."

In a sense everyone who believes in Christ and receives him as Lord and Savior is also a gambler. We are called by him to risk, yet each of us is summoned to bet his or her life on higher stakes. We bet our life on the One whose name is above every name. Faith in him may be a gamble. We see the wrong in the universe but we still believe truth triumphs in the end.

The Christian dares to hold firm to a faith that teaches:

> Though the cause of evil prosper,
> Yet 'tis truth alone is strong;
> Though her portion be the scaffold,
> And upon the throne be wrong;
> Yet that scaffold sways the future,
> And, behind the dim unknown,
> Standeth God within the shadow
> Keeping watch above his own.
> *James Russell Lowell*

It takes great willingness to trust the promises of God, to take him at his word, to risk high stakes against seemingly terrible odds in what becomes the gamble of faith. Not even Jesus could see beyond Calvary, yet undergirding him was a faith that God would be beyond Calvary, and, believing that, he took a chance. And he won.

The Christian today must be willing to take the risk, to bet life on a God who snatched victory out of defeat and who took the consummate atrocity of history and presented humanity its greatest gift.

Amid the pain and misery of our own time, the bitter fruits of life's twisted motives and ignorance, the deficiencies that distort us and our society, the Christian gambles for higher stakes. For we believe that "God so loved the world that he gave his only Son, that whoever believes in him should not perish but have eternal life" (John 3:16). We stake our lives on him who took the sting out of death and snatched victory from the grave.

Beyond that brutal scene at Golgotha, the cross and the crap game—we stand to affirm the testimony of the hardened Roman centurion, proved true by two thousand years of history: "Truly, this man was the Son of God!"

And you can bet your life on him!

But on the first day of the week, at early dawn, they went to the tomb, taking the spices which they had prepared. And they found the stone rolled away from the tomb, but when they went in they did not find the body. While they were perplexed about this, behold, two men stood by them in dazzling apparel; and as they were frightened and bowed their faces to the ground, the men said to them, "Why do you seek the living among the dead? Remember how he told you, while he was still in Galilee, that the Son of man must be delivered into the hands of sinful men, and be crucified, and on the third day rise." And they remembered his words, and returning from the tomb they told all this to the eleven and to all the rest. Now it was Mary Magdalene and Joanna and Mary, the mother of James, and the other women with them who told this to the apostles; but these words seemed to them an idle tale, and they did not believe them **(Luke 24:1-12)**.

Good News from a Graveyard!

It had been a week of great expectations and even greater disappointments. The Galilean, hailed the victor on Palm Sunday, would suffer the agonizing tortures of a criminal before week's end.

He ruffled some ecclesiastical feathers when he chased the money changers from the Temple. He shocked the disciples, his inner circle of friends, when he cursed the fig tree. He had a climactic, memorable Passover meal on Thursday night in a borrowed upper room amid bickering disciples jockeying for position and prominence in the coming Kingdom. Because of that evening, his followers in future generations would see a towel and a basin, bread and wine as symbolic examples of the servant and his sacrifice.

In the Garden of Gethsemane, Peter, his most vocal spokesman, tried to help the cause by swiftly seizing the sword. In return all he got was a reprimand from Jesus. In swift succession, there follow the traitor's kiss, a quick arrest, and a farcical trial before the high priest, Caiaphas. Then, the fickle crowd yelling for Barabbas, the sentence by Pilate, and the denial by Peter. Jesus is mocked and scourged.

On a hill outside Jerusalem, this carpenter from Nazareth, condemned by the Roman procurator of Judea and the high priest of the Jews, was hanged upon a cross.

The burnished dream ended in a bloody nightmare. Darkness covered the earth, the veil of the Temple was "rent in twain." The splendid hope was now a mangled despair. The voice was silenced! Jesus' dead body, nailed to a cruel tree, hung between two thieves. Before sunset this body was laid in a borrowed grave. Jesus of Nazareth, king of the Jews, was now a dead king.

These are the facts. Let no person attempt to sugarcoat them. But the drama moves to Sunday and the first Easter!

No event in the New Testament, indeed no event in the ancient world, is better attested to than the resurrection of Jesus from the dead. Four historians recorded this story in overwhelming detail in their four Gospels. The resurrection is affirmed in twenty-three of twenty-seven books in the New Testament. And it became the keystone of the faith, the central sermon preached by the early church: "Christ has died, Christ is risen, Christ will come again!"

Since that first Easter, Jesus' followers have defied all reason to proclaim that the Jew of Nazareth is the Son of God. By dying for humanity's sin, he reconciled the world to its Creator and gave the world its Redeemer.

This is the reason Easter is good news and has been the crowning festival day of the Christian Year for almost twenty centuries. Christianity has always been content to stand or fall by this paradox, this mystery, this unfathomable truth. Christ died, was buried, and on the third day, he rose again! Dying, he destroyed our death; rising, he restored our life.

People may talk about springtime and new life, flowers and the greening of God's good earth, Easter eggs and bunny rabbits, myths, and symbols, but that is not the Easter proclamation.

Easter rests on one particular story: a quite specific drama about one Man—not a myth—ordered crucified by the Roman governor, Pontius Pilate, and reported to have risen from the grave. This is the "Good News from a Graveyard!"

Early in the morning on the first day of the week, three women—Mary Magdalene, Joanna, and Mary, mother of James—came through the half-light of that morn with spices in hand to anoint the dead body of Jesus. They had not come to the tomb on Saturday because it was the Jewish Sabbath and to have done so would have broken the Jewish law. The ancient custom was to visit the tomb of a loved one three days after death. The belief was that for three days, the spirit of the dead person hovered and waited at the tomb. Only after then did the spirit depart, for the body had by then become unrecognizable through decay.

On the way, the women questioned among themselves, "Who will roll the stone away?" Luke says the women found the stone already rolled away, and the body missing. Two men in gleaming clothes asked, "Why are you looking among the dead for one who is alive? He is not here; he has been raised" (Luke 24:5-6a GNB).

This is the *good news from the graveyard!* "He is risen!"

For three centuries we are told that the Christian people greeted one another, "The Lord is risen" to which the greeted person would answer, "The Lord is risen, indeed." This was no mere "good morning," or "how are you?"

This is the message of Easter, the story of the risen, victorious Christ in whose victory we may share. The curtain came down at Calvary but it rose again on a new scene on Easter Day. It is continuous, this last act. That day a chapter of history began that continues to this day. The subject of this unique event is God, not man, and only God can know the full truth of this historic event. Our only road to the understanding of this divine act is through faith—faith in the reality and truth of what the Evangelists so variously described.

The cross is central, forever central, to the Christian gospel. But the cross is not the climax. The symbol of our faith is not a crucifix, a dead Christ upon the cross. The symbol of our faith is the empty cross on which the Lord of Glory was slain but from which he came down when he had conquered evil and destroyed its power forever.

E. Stanley Jones, the great twentieth-century missionary, wrote that a Muslim taunted a Christian, saying whereas they had the tomb of the prophet as a place of pilgrimage, the Christians had no certain burial place that they knew for sure was the tomb of Jesus. Quickly and quietly came Stanley Jones' reply, "We have no tomb because we have no corpse."

No tomb! No corpse! We have the living Christ instead.

Michelangelo, it is said, reproached his fellow painters, "Why do you paint Christ on the cross so often? Christ suffering; Christ dying; Christ dead. Paint him, rather, risen! with his foot upon the rock; paint him victorious and glorious; paint him the conqueror of sin and death!" Crown him with many crowns!

> Crown him the Lord of life,
> Who triumphed o'er the grave,
> And rose victorious in the strife
> For those he came to save;
> His glories now we sing
> Who died, and rose on high,
> Who died, eternal life to bring,
> And lives, that death may die.
> *Matthew Bridges and Godfrey Thring*

Too many Christians get as far as Good Friday and Calvary and remain there. The Christian way of life, they would have us believe, is a grim, tough, tragic, and tearful business in this world of sin and woe. To them nothing ultimately matters.

If the brightest light that man has ever known can be snuffed out by the culture of Greece, the law of Rome, and the pressures of a noble monotheistic tradition, what hope is there? All is vanity. We fall into what Paul Goodman describes as the "Nothing-can-be-done-disease." Despair is the only response.

No such thing! Life is a glorious adventure, under the triumphant leadership of the all-conquering Christ. *Why is it that some Christians try to carry that which should lift them?*

Charles Wesley, that singing troubadour of Methodism, uses the present tense in his magnificently moving hymn, "O for a Thousand Tongues to Sing." Listen to Wesley:

> Jesus! the name that *charms* our fears,
> That *bids* our sorrows cease,
> 'Tis music in the sinners' ears,
> 'Tis life, and health, and peace.
>
> He *breaks* the power of canceled sin,
> He sets the prisoner free; . . .
>
> He *speaks*, and listening to his voice,
> New life the dead receive; . . .
>
> *Hear* him, ye deaf; his praise, ye dumb,
> Your loosened tongues employ;
> Ye blind, behold your Savior *come;*
> And *leap*, ye lame, for joy.
>
> (italics added)

He is quite right; Jesus *is* present and *does* that now! Today!

The Christian religion was born through sorrow and suffering. It was cradled in adversity and suckled on hardship and sacrifice. At the very heart of it is a cross and a suffering Savior. Let never pass unchallenged the heresy that says that the Christian faith is a gospel of prosperity and health. The faith we proclaim does not ignore, evade, or make light of suffering and sorrow. The joyful faith and optimism of Christians mean we know that the dread issues of life and death have been met and

82

conquered in the cross and in the resurrection of Jesus Christ.

"He is not here; for he has risen, as he said" (Matt. 28:6).

Easter is more than an empty tomb. It was not the unoccupied grave that convinced the disciples that Jesus had been raised from the dead; it was their *continued experience of his presence beyond the crucifixion.*

Jesus is not only what he said and did during his brief ministry, but what he accomplished by his suffering, death, and subsequent resurrection from the dead. By his death and resurrection he did what man alone could never do—he restored between God and his children the fellowship that had been broken by man's rebellion and perpetuated by man's sin.

Look at the contrast in two pictures painted in the Gospels.

The first one follows.

On the night after Calvary in an upper room in Jerusalem, a group of men are cowering behind bolted and barricaded doors. Their faces reflect their fear. Even more, each one of them is marked with dejection: hopeless, final, irretrievable dejection. They are dazed, stunned, bewildered. They sit in silence, too heartbroken to speak, too benumbed in soul to pray. Everything is at an end. There is nothing to live for. They were at the point that the creed would later put it, "He was crucified, dead, and buried." Period. Not only was Jesus dead, his movement was dead. And against its tomb a great stone of despair had been rolled. This is the first picture.

Here is the second.

Seven weeks later we see the same group of men. They are not hiding behind closed doors now. They are out in the streets, aflame with a superhuman confidence. They are absolutely fearless and overwhelmingly happy. They are planning the conquest of the earth. By A.D. 70 all the apostles, except John, were dead. Tradition tells us all died martyrs' deaths.

83

Look at the two pictures. One is blasted hope; the other is hope blasting the world. One is a ruined remnant; the other, the nucleus of a marching, militant church. What a startling, incredible change had occurred in these men's lives! Can we explain it? Yes! Between the two pictures in the briefest span of time, something happened. "He is not here! He is risen!" That is our good news from a graveyard. Christ is risen indeed!

Every effect must have an adequate cause and the cause that turned cowards into heroes was the resurrection. The church was founded on this good news. Without the risen Lord, the church would have never existed. Many times it has seemed doomed or dead. From the time of the Roman emperors to our time of Lenin and Stalin and Mao Tse-tung the gravediggers have been busy burying the church, but always it has broken open the tomb and tolled the stone away.

I read an interesting, almost bizarre item. In a cemetery in Germany, is a tombstone made of huge slabs of granite and riveted together with strong steel clasps. On the stone these words are carved in German, "This burial place must never be opened. It covers the grave of a woman who believed in no resurrection for anybody and she ordered that her grave be made secure." But something happened. A little tiny seed chanced to lie between the stones. It began to make little roots and push out a little into the light, and almost as if the universe were laughing, a growing tree has wrenched the steel clasps about and has pushed out the stones to make room for life.

The Christian in whose heart the Lord Christ already lives knows that those who believe and serve the risen Savior will never die. Let me tell you of one contemporary Christian.

Daniel Lord, a Jesuit priest, learned at age sixty-six he

was incurably ill with cancer of both lungs. He was asked by a radio talk show host how he felt about it and we can well ponder his reply:

> When I first got word of incurable cancer early this year, I must admit that I got the feeling of relief.
>
> Some diseases I couldn't have the patience to bear, but cancer is not one of them. By learning the true facts early, I was given an opportunity to clean up a lot of unfinished work and to see friends whom I have been neglecting.
>
> Then, too, I suddenly found that life became very precious. The world looked good and time became so valuable that I tried to squeeze every second I could from every hour. I became more acutely aware of everything.
>
> If, for me, the end of life on earth was really the end of the road, I suppose I would dread it, but I don't believe it is. I think it is only the beginning of a more abundant life.

He could give such an answer about death because of the quality and depth of his faith in the risen Lord.

Because he lives in my heart, I cannot but believe that God's purposes will ultimately prevail. Service will triumph over exploitation; generosity will triumph over greed; freedom will triumph over bondage; grace will triumph over sin; and love will be victorious over hate.

In the light of the Easter triumph, we keep busy with our Father's business here on earth. As Paul said, "We are afflicted in every way, but not crushed; perplexed, but not driven to despair; persecuted, but not forsaken; struck down, but not destroyed" (II Cor. 4:8-9).

On that first Easter Sunday, God turned it all around. God sent his creation, good news from a graveyard. Well may our hearts be glad as we continue to do his work and make it our own.

In 1981, the late Dr. Harrell Beck closed his Bible study at the Centennial Conference of World Methodism in Hawaii with a poignant, moving episode from the life of Giacomo Puccini. Puccini! What a great man he was!

He wrote *Madame Butterfly, La Bohème, La Tosca.* What fluent melodic writing and bold dramatic harmonies from this incredible man!

In 1922 he was stricken with cancer. He said, "I want to write one more opera." So, he sat down to write *Turandot.* His students said, "But suppose you die?"

"Oh," Puccini replied, "my disciples will finish it. Never care."

In 1924 he died and his disciples did finish his music. Its première was held in Milan, Italy, at La Scala Opera House, under the baton of Puccini's best student, Arturo Toscanini. The gala performance proceeded and came to that point in the music where the composer had laid down his pen. Tears streamed down Toscanini's face. He put down the baton and turned to the audience and said, "Thus far, the master wrote . . . and then the master died."

Then picking up his baton, his face wreathed with smiles, Toscanini shouted out to the audience, "But his disciples finished his music."

Will we? Will we finish the work begun by our Master? I pray God we will.

"He is not here. He is risen."

Jesus surely knew the Scriptures. The prophet Jeremiah said, "Let not the rich man gloat in his riches, nor the wise man snide over his wisdom, let him who glories glory in this: that the Lord God delights in kindness, in justice, in righteousness."

The gift of incompleted work was given so that we might become that word of God made flesh in our world, in our time, in this place.

He is not here. He is risen! He is risen indeed! This is *the good news from a graveyard.*

That very day two of them were going to a village named Emmaus, about seven miles from Jerusalem, and talking with each other about all these things that had happened. While they were talking and discussing together, Jesus himself drew near and went with them. But their eyes were kept from recognizing him. . . .

So they drew near to the village to which they were going. He appeared to be going further, but they constrained him, saying, "Stay with us, for it is toward evening and the day is now far spent." So he went in to stay with them. When he was at table with them, he took the bread and blessed, and broke it, and gave it to them. And their eyes were opened and they recognized him; and he vanished out of their sight. They said to each other, "Did not our hearts burn within us while he talked to us on the road, while he opened to us the scriptures?" And they rose that same hour and returned to Jerusalem; and they found the eleven gathered together and those who were with them, who said, "The Lord has risen indeed, and has appeared to Simon!" Then they told what had happened on the road, and how he was known to them in the breaking of the bread (**Luke 24:13-16, 28-35**).

On the Road Again!

When I made my first pilgrimage to Israel, I asked an Arab Christian—whose Palestinian ancestry can be traced for more than a thousand years in that ancient land—if there was any place in the Holy Land where I could be reasonably assured of walking where Jesus had walked.

I had been skeptical, you see, about American pilgrims who go the Holy Land, come back with slides and script, and declare, "I walked where Jesus walked!" Two thousand years of shifting sands, the destruction of the biblical city of Jerusalem, the construction of modern roads, and other changes in the name of progress had convinced me that such certainty was difficult, if not impossible.

Quickly, the Palestinian Christian responded, "There are two places where I am personally convinced you can do just that! One is the steps leading to the Church of the Cockcrow. The other is the old road in the village of Emmaus. That stone remnant, built by the Romans long before Jesus was born, is still intact today alongside the village church." In a loving gesture of hospitality he said, "I'll take you there."

On the way I learned there are two Emmaus villages in the Holy Land. One, spoken of by Josephus, the Jewish historian, is some four miles from Jerusalem. The other is off the Jaffa Road, and here we arrived late on a Sunday afternoon. We entered the courtyard of the church and then walked onto the excavated Roman–Byzantine road flanked by the ruins of the historic wine vats and oil presses. "The wine in this village was so famous," he said, "that people came from as far away as Spain to buy it." Whether or not this was the actual place of our story, the setting certainly would have been similar.

One of the immortal short stories in the body of Christian literature is set on that historic road. Luke alone records the story of the two persons trudging homeward along a sunset road to a village called Emmaus.

Luke says two followers of Jesus walked along this road—perplexed, baffled, sad, and dispirited. The bottom had dropped out of their world. They had placed their hopes in Jesus as "the one to redeem Israel" (Luke 24:21b). And now the prophet's voice was silent. Jesus was dead and their dearest hopes had crumbled into despair!

They had lingered in Jerusalem for two whole days, hoping for some better news. All they heard was idle rumor.

Earlier that morning women had gone to anoint the body of Jesus but found only an empty tomb. They rushed back to tell "the eleven and the rest" what they had seen, but "the story seemed to them to be nonsense and they would not believe them" (Luke 24:11 Goodspeed).

The story of the empty tomb *was* incredible. Now they walked along, heavy-hearted, rehearsing the events that surrounded Jesus' death.

I find their reaction quite normal. Today when a loved one dies, family and friends are found telling and retelling the events that happened prior to the death.

Suddenly, a Stranger approaches and walks beside them. "Absorbed in their serious talk and discussion," as J. B. Phillips puts it, they were amazed that this

89

Stranger, who fell in step alongside them, appeared to know little or nothing of the events that so totally engrossed them. His quizzical tone and apparent ignorance of the recent happenings in Jerusalem puzzled them. To the unrecognized and risen Lord they said, "How can you possibly have been in Jerusalem during these last few days without knowing what happened?"

The Stranger, wanting to draw them out more, asked, "What do you mean?" So they proceeded to tell him why they were downcast and troubled. They spoke to him of Jesus of Nazareth, a prophet strong in word and deed, whom they expected to deliver Israel from her present occupation by Rome and to usher in the kingdom of God. This Jesus had been crucified and buried. And now rumor had reached his followers that the tomb was empty. Some said he had risen from the dead.

The unknown Wayfarer chided them for their slowness to believe the full message of the prophets since they did not really understand their Scriptures. He began "with Moses," that is, the first five books of the Bible traditionally ascribed to Moses, and "all the prophets" of the Old Testament and explained how "all the scriptures" contained things concerning himself.

By twilight they had reached their destination, the village of Emmaus. With typical Middle East hospitality, they invited the traveling Stranger to lodge with them, for it was evening now and night travel might be difficult and dangerous. "So he went in to stay with them."

Now, it is interesting to note that in the Middle East it is customary for the host to seat himself at the head of the table, bless the meal, take the bread, break it, and share it with those about the table. On this occasion Jesus—unasked—assumed the role of host. He took the loaf, blessed it, and gave it to them.

It is quite possible there was something familiar in his

manner of taking, breaking, and distributing the bread that revealed to his two companions who their guest really was.

"Their eyes were opened and they recognized him." But he did not stay with them. He vanished out of their sight. They remembered then how he set their hearts aflame as he interpreted the Scriptures to them while they walked.

The two were compelled to return to Jerusalem without delay to share the momentous experience with the apostles. Even before they could report what had happened to them, their hearts rejoiced to hear: "The Lord has risen indeed, and has appeared to Simon!" The two then related their own story of returning to Emmaus and being joined on the road by the Stranger whom, in the breaking of the bread, they recognized as the risen Lord!

This classic story is not the stuff of imagination. Rather, it is a simple narrative with a surprising revelation: two of his avowed followers *did not recognize him* even though they had been personally involved with this Carpenter from Galilee.

As disciples of Jesus, they were thinking and talking about the puzzling events that had occurred during Passover. Now, on the road again, they are sick at heart, sad, and filled with disappointment. *Yes, they heard the story of the empty tomb but they didn't get the message!* As one translator described them, "Their faces were drawn with misery."

How many of us can identify with these two? Do we hope in Christ and believe he is our liberator, the one to deliver us from whatever bondage possesses us? Out of life's circumstances that lead to disappointment and doubt, do we often choose to return to the familiar scenes of our past, letting go of our faith and hope in the future?

We hear the story, we get the facts, but tragically, like the Emmaus pair, we don't "get the message." Many of us are blessed with a good Christian background. We learned our catechism. We can recite the books of the Bible, spouting Scripture passages like a fountain. We know Bible history, Bible geography, Bible names. But, it all means little or nothing. The tragic truth is we fail to grasp the *true meaning* of the events or the *significance* of such encounters for ourselves and others.

Jesus' crucifixion is easily accepted in our religious search for a faith. We look upon him as a martyr who goes nobly to a death he did not deserve. Our understanding of his life and teachings, however, ceases to grow beyond the figure of the crucified Jesus. There we stop. We go no further. The rest of the story sounds like an idle tale. Our experience with Jesus find us on that road again, wondering.

Christ's presence is never casually realized. Cleopas and Simon would never have discovered him to be alive if they had not been both passionately hoping for the coming of his kingdom and devastated by the loss of his presence.

Scripture records make clear that the risen Christ was seen only by those devoted to him—those within his circle of friends. There is no account of the general public or any of his adversaries having seen him. However, the sight of the risen Lord did not produce the disciples' faith. Rather, it was the inner and lasting assurance of his presence with them that gave these disciples, and humanity, faith in the reality of the living Christ.

Those of us who remain faithful to him, despite the disappointments and doubts of daily life, know that where two or three are gathered in his name, he is there in our midst.

Often our eyes "may be kept from recognizing him." Whether this is due to our own blindness or God's intention is not the issue. "We walk by faith, not by sight." In the last analysis, I believe, the resurrection appearances give birth to new faith. The theologian G.

E. Ladd suggests the apostles had "lost faith" but the resurrection "created faith."

Why are sermons on the Emmaus story and other appearances of our risen Lord so seldom heard in our churches today? We make a great deal of the earthly life of Jesus. Our interest in him from Advent through Christmas and Epiphany intensifies during Lent. Our activity in the church and worship builds to a grand climax on Easter Sunday.

The Sunday after Easter is called Low Sunday. In the church today we typically find the rank and file who have followed Jesus to Jerusalem for forty days, thereafter tending to ignore their resurrected Lord. The resurrection is properly acknowledged but then in far too many congregations the Christian and church activity significantly diminishes. There is little sense of celebration again until the coming Advent.

Have the events whereby the resurrection was confirmed become our stumbling block? Has our faith been reduced to a religiosity that appreciates Jesus and his example yet gives scant emphasis to the appearances of the risen Savior? Have we reduced the Passion story to shallow religious sentiment? Do we live out our faith in such well meaning ways as: a father's devotion to the family, a mother's complete submission to the needs of a child, a son's or daughter's care for aging parents, a person's service to his civic club or community or commitment to his or her job?

Do we equate these levels of living, however admirable, with authentic Christianity? Does our faith take us no further than the crucifixion? Is what lies beyond embarrassing? In our scientific and technological age have we little need for a risen Savior?

How sad! Precisely here, the distinctive character of the Christian faith begins to emerge. The experience of the first-century Christians cannot be summed up adequately in terms of Jesus' moral teachings, exemplary life, and sacrificial death. The early Christians experienced something more, though their understanding at the time was only fragmentary.

Perhaps our trouble is we read these Gospel passages as reports of the last stages of Jesus' earthly life—a series of strung-out farewells—the afterglow to earthly ministry.

These appearances are not curtain calls after the drama of redemption has been played out. They are the opening scenes of a new drama and, yes, even a new world.

The appearances do not restore the earthly Jesus. Rather, they reveal our eternal Christ. Nothing is more notable in the early Christians' faith than the firm, steadfast assurance of their ultimate destiny.

Their belief is expressed in the Epistle of John: "Beloved, we are God's children now; it does not yet appear what we shall be, but we know that when he appears we shall be like him, for we shall see him as he is" (I John 3:2).

Biblically we are not to judge ourselves in terms of our present imperfections. Rather, we are to understand our true nature in terms of a wholeness and holiness yet to be ours. The promise of Jesus was made not only to a dying, repentant thief but to all who follow the risen Savior— "You will be with me in Paradise" (Luke 23:43b).

A call to prayer is often sung in many churches today. It is a plea to God: "Open our eyes, Lord, we want to see Jesus— to reach our and touch him—and tell him we love him."

If the resurrection is to be real to the modern Christian, the prayer voiced in that song needs to become your prayer and my prayer. "Open my eyes, Lord, I want to see Jesus."

There is the story of a Bohemian painter who lived on a houseboat. It is told in the film *The Horse's Mouth*. A young admirer of the artist asks why and how he became a painter. The man, looking out through a broken window as though at something far away, says,

"One time I saw a painting, by Matisse, in brilliant color, as though for the first time. It skinned my eyes; I became a different person, it was like a conversion!" *Think about that!*

My eyes were skinned! I became a different person! It lifted the veil from my seeing! I saw things differently—in color—and dimension—and meaning!

You and I need such a moment of revelation.

The Emmaus travelers, on the road again, did not recognize Jesus. Humanly speaking, their failure to recognize the Lord resembles many modern skeptics, found in the church today, who are convinced such miracles do not happen!

Could it be that we, like them, suffer a disease not of the eyes or of the ears? Our inability to recognize him may be, instead, a disease of the heart. We have the witness of the Word but our hearts are not in tune with the resurrected Lord. It is easy and safe to keep a dead Jesus in his tomb.

There's a telling story about an irate parishioner who abruptly stopped her minister one Sunday morning and said, "Pastor, if Jesus knew what was going on in this congregation, he would be turning over in his grave!" Now there's an interesting theology of the resurrection! Have we persistently, like her, kept Jesus in the grave?

Two dispirited followers met Jesus. On the road again, their eyes were opened.

Albert Schweitzer reminds us:

> He comes to us as One unknown, without a name, as of old, by the lake-side, He came to those men who knew Him not. He speaks to us the same word: "Follow thou me!" and sets us to the tasks which He has to fulfil for our time. He commands. And to those who obey Him, whether they be wise or simple, He will reveal Himself in the toils, the conflicts, the sufferings which they shall pass through in His fellowship, and, as an ineffable mystery, they shall learn in their own experience Who He is.[1]

He is Lord! He is alive! He is here! Look around!

And behold, a lawyer stood up to put him to the test, saying, "Teacher, what shall I do to inherit eternal life?" He said to him, "What is written in the law? How do you read?" And he answered, "You shall love the Lord your God with all your heart, and with all your soul, and with all your strength, and with all your mind; and your neighbor as yourself." And he said to him, "You have answered right; do this, and you will live."

But he, desiring to justify himself, said to Jesus, "And who is my neighbor?" Jesus replied, "A man was going down from Jerusalem to Jericho, and he fell among robbers, who stripped him and beat him, and departed, leaving him half dead. Now by chance a priest was going down that road; and when he saw him he passed by on the other side. So likewise a Levite, when he came to the place and saw him, passed by on the other side. But a Samaritan, as he journeyed, came to where he was; and when he saw him, he had compassion, and went to him and bound up his wounds, pouring on oil and wine; then he set him on his own beast and brought him to an inn, and took care of him. And the next day he took out two denarii and gave them to the innkeeper, saying, 'Take care of him; and whatever more you spend, I will repay you when I come back.' Which of these three, do you think, proved neighbor to the man who fell among the robbers?" He said, "The one who showed mercy on him." And Jesus said to him, "Go and do likewise" **(Luke 10:25-37).**

"A new commandment I give unto you, that you love one another; even as I have loved you, that you also love one another" **(John 13:34).**

The Bottom Line

One of the most common phrases heard in the marketplace is "the bottom line." It makes no difference whether we are purchasing a car, a house, a new wardrobe, or planning a vacation; we count the cost. We want to know. "What's the bottom line?" In measuring the cost of our economic and social life the extent of our investment is determined, primarily, by that "bottom line."

Is there also a bottom line in our religion? Perhaps you never thought of it exactly that way, but consider the question with me today. To discover an answer, let us turn first to what many consider to be the greatest short story in the Gospels.

One day a certain expert in the law came to Jesus and asked him a question about the bottom line in religion. What is the great priority in human experience? When all is said and done, what is most important about life? So the lawyer asked: "What shall I do to inherit eternal life?" An honest question. A sincere question. Jesus answered him in terms of what the lawyer already knew, "What is written in the law? How do you read?"

Jesus knew that the lawyer, like any strict orthodox Jew, probably wore a little leather box called a phylactery on his wrist. Was he saying, "You have the answer on your wrist before you, look at it? There's the answer to your question." These phylacteries contained certain passages from the books of Jewish Law. So the lawyer, answered, "You must love the Lord your God with all your heart, with all your soul, and with all your strength, and with all your mind, and your neighbor as yourself" (Luke 10:27 JB). Jesus told him, "You already know that is the answer. Do this, and you shall live."

Then comes the barbed question from the lawyer, desiring to justify himself, "Who is my neighbor?" Some have viewed this inquiry as a lawyer trying to set a trap for Jesus. Instead let us look at it as perhaps life's most significant question?

Consider the setting.

In that ancient Jewish world the Jewish law itself declared that the Jews had no responsibility for those outside the circle of their own people. The Jew did not regard the Gentile as a neighbor. Some held, in fact, that it was illegal to assist a Gentile woman in childbirth, for doing so would be to bring yet another Gentile into the world.[1] The Greek world looked at those outside its own nationality as barbarians. So as Jesus summarizes the law as love for God and neighbor—the bottom line—the lawyer quizzically asks, "Okay, but who is my neighbor?"

Jesus, responded, as so often was his custom, by telling a story. This story is the famous parable of the good Samaritan, in which a Jewish traveler is beaten, stripped, robbed, and left for dead along the Jericho road. A priest came by, looked at him, then walked on the other side of the road. Then a Levite came upon the stricken man. He looked at him but also passed him by. Finally, a Samaritan—a half breed, a person of mixed blood, a social and religious outcast—came by, saw him, and was moved with compassion. He tenderly bound up his wounds, picked him up, put him on his donkey, and took him to the nearest inn. The next day he paid the innkeeper to look after him and promised, "Whatever more you are out of pocket, when I come back this way, I'll square up with you in full."

Apparently, the Samaritan was frequently a guest at the inn and had good credit, along with some practical religion. At least he was trustworthy. The priest and the Levite were so busy playing at their religion that they didn't have time to be religious.

Jesus asked the lawyer, "Which of these three do you think, proved neighbor to the man who fell among robbers?" And the lawyer answered, "The one who had mercy on him."

"Go and do likewise," Jesus counseled.

The "bottom line!"

Jesus came to tell us that the bottom line in religion is to love God and love neighbor. This story can be interpreted as a moral example of the neighborliness expected of Christians—as it often is in sermons. Some scholars see the parable as a paradox designed to transmit Jesus' special understanding of what God demands of everyone who would truly do his will.

John Dominic Crossan, an expert in parable analysis at DePaul University in Chicago says, "In this parable Jesus is asking his Jewish audience to think the unthinkable by identifying goodness with the hated Samaritan."

Not only did Jesus tell us this story but he showed us that God's love is a special kind of love. His is a kind of love that looks beyond the gate, scans the horizon, watching, waiting, and hoping for the return of a wandering child. God's love is like a shepherd's who counts ninety-nine sheep safely in the sheepfold but goes out in the night searching, searching for the one missing sheep. Throughout Jesus' three-year ministry he continually demonstrated that love is the bottom line.

This reveals the difference between our God and the god of some other religions. We do not need to beg our Father to do right by us, he is already doing right by us. The Christian's task is to become aware, to open up, and to respond to God's loving call. Since God is love, nothing can happen to us—here or hereafter—that will cause God to stop loving us.

The greatest difficulty Jesus had on earth, I believe, was to convince people that God loves us and wants us to love one another. Two thousand years later, let us admit, it is still our greatest challenge.

Who is my neighbor?

Jesus gave no abstract or pious answer. He took his questioner on the road of life and showed him a practical act of neighborliness.

What does it mean to be a neighbor? You will notice one strange thing in the whole story of the good Samaritan: the one person in the drama about whom we know nothing personal is the poor man who was befriended. The moral and religious character of the others is plainly set forth. The robbers characterize the bad guys. The priest and the Levite are pious men who lack the milk of human kindness. The Samaritan, a heretic in the eyes of the religious community, is the man with compassion who helped the poor fellow. The Gospel writer tells us nothing about the man who was helped. Was he good or bad? Heretic or pious? Jew or Samaritan? Greek or Roman? Wealthy or poor? We don't know. He was just a man who went down the road from Jerusalem to Jericho and fell among robbers. The only description Jesus gives is: a man.

This man represents every person lying helpless by the side of life's open roads. He has no face, no nationality, no color of skin, no particular creed, no religious affiliation. He is every person and any person in need.

Jesus, nevertheless, put his finger on the basic requirement of life when he accepts this quote from the Pentateuch as answering the question truthfully: "You must love the Lord your God with all your heart . . . soul . . . strength . . . and mind . . . and your neighbor as yourself." The bottom line of the Christian's goal is to translate this command to love into the stuff of daily life.

The meaning of love, as used in the Gospels, is not romantic emotionalism but rather a warm, caring concern for other persons. The word "love" is woven into the fabric of the New Testament:

> Dear friends, let us love one another, because love comes from God. Whoever loves is a child of God and knows God. Whoever does not love does not know God, for God is love. . . .
>
> And we ourselves know and believe the love which God has for us. . . .
>
> There is no fear in love; perfect love drives out all fear. So then, love has not been made perfect in anyone who is afraid, because fear has to do with punishment.
>
> We love because God first loved us. If someone says he loves God, but hates his brother, he is a liar. For he cannot love God, whom he has not seen, if he does not love his brother, whom he has seen. The command that Christ has given us is this: whoever loves God must love his brother also (I John 4:7-6, 16, 18-21 GNB).

Yet love is more than a word or words! Jesus is the supreme gift of God's love to us. To say "God is love" may, or may not, convey much meaning to the average person in today's world. But to say that God "loved the world so much that he gave his only Son" is to confront the world with the act of a living, caring God who pours out his love in a personal way that each and every individual in his earthly family might be touched.

If God is going to bring order out of our chaotic human predicament, healing out of our fears and hatreds, and wholeness to the human race, we need to accept, mediate, and reflect this unconditional love. In Jesus the law of perfect love became the gospel of God's grace; the law of love was fulfilled in the life of love. This love alone mirrors what the Bible calls the grace of God.

His grace is indiscriminately poured out to bring healing and reconciliation among the families of man. By that I mean that "God loved *the world*"—not just the good people, the religious people, the American people, but all the people in the whole world.

God's love has never played favorites. He is not selectively kind and generous. Whereas we may choose to discriminate, welcoming those whom we like or those to whom we feel obligated, God loves all—even those whom we may see as the least lovable or least deserving within the human family.

Jesus, only once, laid down a commandment for his disciples. I am not speaking of his teachings or the principles of faith upon which Christianity rests; I speak of his commandment. In one sense, it is Jesus' farewell word to the apostles. He warns the Twelve that he must leave them shortly to go on that journey which he must walk alone. Lest they fail to understand what is his distinctive teaching, he lays before them a new commandment: "That you love one another; even as I have loved you."

The word for humanity today, the bottom line, if you will, is simply this: love or perish. We cannot afford to hate or to think of love as some sweet sentimentality.

In the words of Aldous Huxley, who held no brief for Christianity:

> Of all the worn, smudged, dog's-eared words in our vocabulary, "love" is surely the grubbiest, smelliest, slimiest. Bawled from a million pulpits, lasciviously crooned through hundreds of millions of loud-speakers, it has become an outrage to good taste, and decent feeling, an obscenity which one hesitates to pronounce. And yet it has to be pronounced, for, after all, Love is the last word.[2]

To be Christian means nothing less than taking seriously the commandment of Jesus, "That you love one another; even as I have loved you."

The Christian knows that love is the only thing that makes life worth the living, and that when one does love, one does forget oneself. The difference precisely between a Christian and one who does not profess Christ as Savior is not that the one is unselfish and the other is selfish. Clearly the difference is that a Christian is one who dares to truly care about other people and to express care and love for them without much concern about being loved in return.

The point, I believe, of the story of the good Samaritan is that Jesus is saying, "I don't know who your neighbor is but as you walk the road of life, if you really take these principles to heart and make them practical, you will find out who he is; you will recognize him. If you walk with open eyes and a warm heart, if you really look about you at the suffering, torn world, you'll find out who your neighbor is, you will see him. You may find him by the side of the road, set upon by robbers or gangs; or you may discover him in the pain and suffering welling up in the eyes of a neighbor. I cannot tell you exactly who your neighbor is. I can only show you how loving God and loving your neighbor works out in daily life."

This is the bottom line! This is the most pointed story in all the Gospels, it is the most beautiful, it never grows old.

This parable, however, has pricked the conscience of its hearers ever since Jesus first told it. It still works out this way: each one must personally interpret the parable, in terms of daily experiences, discovering what Jesus really means. For each person it will mean something uniquely different.

This kind of love has moved millions to share with the hungry and the homeless. This is the kind of love and level of love that has sent some people out of their comfort and seclusion into slums and ghettos to serve the poor and live among them. This is a love that has motivated the greatest missionaries to go to hot jungles or frigid wastelands to serve God's children there in the name of Christ. This is a love that alone gives the promise of breaking down the barriers of race and creed and gives humanity hope for peace.

Christ not only talked of such love and commanded it but he demonstrated it. The world, however, was not ready to accept his way of love as a way of life. To reveal the way of love as a way of life was Christ's central mission and ministry. It was a ministry that touched the little children assuring them of their importance. It elevated the status of womanhood far beyond what society in that day was prepared to do. It showed compassion for the mentally and emotionally handicapped as well as for those physically or spiritually ill. It showed a love style as a life-style which lifted human spirits above the selfish interests that often characterize our human nature. The world was not ready for his way of love, became infuriated with him, and crucified him. His way of love is still unpopular in our world but this does not alter the truth of his words, "Greater love hath no man than this, that a man lay down his life for his friend." Christ's love wasn't sentimental; it was self-giving. His adversaries bore the testimony, "He saved others; himself he cannot save." What a truth they spoke! How can one keep what one gives? How can one live for self, when one is living for others?

In the capital city of North Carolina is a hospital named for a retired New England schoolteacher who had taken early retirement because of severe health problems. One day a young divinity student came and asked her to take a job for him because he felt so inadequate for the task. The job was visiting women prisoners in a New England town jail. Dorothea Dix did, and found things she didn't know existed in life. She found the insane mixed among those who were guilty of murder and of misdemeanors. She dedicated the rest of her life doing something for those people who had fallen among thieves and were passed by on the other side of life's road. For forty years, despite her frailness and weak body, she labored, living for others. When she died, she left thirty mental hospitals as monuments to her sense of responsibility for people whom the rest of society looked down upon when they passed by.

Another moving story is told of George Romney's wife. (I'm speaking now of the English painter, not the former governor of Michigan.) As Romney's paintings became known and he achieved widespread recognition, he left home, deserting his wife and children. For thirty-six years he remained in London, having no contact with his wife and family. Finally, a debilitating illness robbed him of his power to paint. Suddenly, remembering his wife, he went back to her. She took him in without complaint and cared for him tenderly until he died.

Romney's biographer says, "That act of love was more significant than any canvas George Romney ever painted." In the loyalty and love of that wife, one can see reflected the love that Jesus talked about.

Only one with the love of Jesus in the heart could have done something like that. And God loves us just like that. Whatever our past rejection of God, whatever the sin of our life, when we turn toward him, he is there.

And that is exactly how Jesus loves us. Why he loves us, God only knows; I don't. I do know that Jesus has shown us, come what may, we can and should hold fast to love. People may break your heart but only you can permit them to embitter or harden your heart. For one, I cannot afford to hate another person. Hatred imprisons; love sets free; and victory comes by forgiveness. To paraphrase Paul in his letter to the church at Rome: "Don't allow yourself to be overpowered by hate. Take the offensive—overpower hate with love" (Rom. 12:21). The overbearing world refuses to exercise such love.

Maybe all this sounds foolhardy to us modern Christians. Perhaps we have yet to learn the new commandment of the Son of God. That is: not simply to love, but to love as Jesus loved. There is a difference, and in that difference we discover life's bottom line.

The loving heart gives, it accepts the risk, it is willing

to sacrifice as Christ loved the church and gave himself for it.

Princess Alice, second daughter of the British monarch, Queen Victoria, had a four-year-old son who contracted the dread disease "black diphtheria," highly contagious and a killer. The princess was frail and was repeatedly warned not to go near her son. One day while standing in a far corner of her child's room, she heard him whisper to a nurse who walked near his bed, "Why doesn't mother kiss me any more?" This was more than she could bear. She raced to the bed, clasped the little one in her arms, and smothered him with kisses—to reassure him of her love. It was the kiss of death. She contracted the disease, and in a matter of weeks both mother and son were buried. She had been willing to risk death because of her love for her son. *There* is the difference—loving *as Jesus loved!*

Loving has a high price tag. It doesn't come cheap. Ask the man of sorrows, acquainted with grief. Go with him to Golgotha. See him on Calvary's cross, held captive by love—love for God and love for all his neighbors.

> See, from his head, his hands, his feet,
> Sorrow and love flow mingled down;
> Did e'er such love and sorrow meet,
> Or thorns compose so rich a crown?
> *Isaac Watts*

Jesus Christ said, "A new commandment I give to you, that you love one another; even as I have loved you."

The cost is high! But nothing cheaper can pay the price of salvation for our world! And that's really the bottom line!

Let us pray:

> Were the whole realm of nature mine,
> That were an offering far too small;
> Love so amazing, so divine,
> Demands my soul, my life, my all. Amen.
> *Isaac Watts*

After this Jesus showed Himself again to the disciples, by the Sea of Tiberias, and this was the way He appeared. There were together Simon Peter and Thomas called the Twin, and Nathanael of Cana in Galilee, the sons of Zebedee and two more of His disciples. Simon Peter said to them, "I am going fishing." They said, "We are coming with you." So they went off and got into the boat, and that night they caught nothing. Day had already dawned when Jesus stood on the shore. The disciples, however, did not know that it was Jesus. Then Jesus said to them, "Boys, have you caught anything?" They answered Him, "No." He told them, "Cast the net to the right of the boat and you will find some." So they cast the net and could not draw it up any more because of the great number of fish.

The disciple whom Jesus loved then said to Peter, "It is the Lord!" So Simon Peter, hearing, "It is the Lord," wrapped his work jacket around him (for he was stripped) and flung himself into the sea. The rest of the disciples came with the boat—for they were near shore, only about a hundred yards away—hauling in the net of fish.

When they got out on land they saw a charcoal fire there with fish on it, and bread. Jesus said to them, "Bring some of the fish you have just caught." Simon Peter got in the boat and hauled the net to shore; it was filled with a hundred and fifty-three large fish, and though there were so many, the net did not tear.

Jesus said to them, "Come and have breakfast." None of the disciples dared ask Him, "Who are You?" for they knew it was the Lord. Jesus came and took the bread and gave it to them, and also the fish. This was the third time Jesus appeared to the disciples after rising from the dead   (John 21:1-14 MLB).

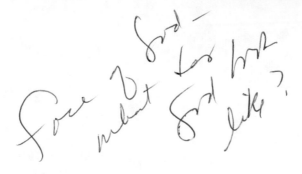

The Real Thing

There is a popular soft drink in America commercially advertised as "the real thing," and I am confident that some people think that particular cola may be the *real* thing. Most Americans search for the real thing in life and despite the consumption of colas, along with a multitude of other drinks, soft and hard, are looking in the wrong places for the real thing.

One of life's greatest tragedies is that we look here and look there and instead of finding the real thing in life, we end up with a substitute or with nothing. That is why our society is infected by a peculiar philosophy that says, "Nothing matters."

Yet, there is a longing in our inner being. It has been expressed by the Psalmist, "As a [deer] longs for flowing streams, so longs my soul for thee, O God" (Ps. 42:1). There is a restlessness expressed by Augustine, "Thou hast made us for thyself, O God, and our souls are restless 'til they find their rest in Thee." There is a loneliness expressed sadly by the French writer Jean Paul Sartre, who, holding no belief in God, reveals what it means to be without God:

> God does not see me, God does not hear me, God does not know me. You see this gap in the door; it is God. You see that hole in the ground; it is God again. Silence is God. Absence is God. God is the loneliness of man.

Millions of folk have decided that what they do and what happens in their world is empty of any meaning.

Helmut Thielicke, in one of his sermons, refers to a modern writer's depiction of this feeling of restive emptiness and nothingness. The writer describes Christ as coming back from the dead and telling the world that there is no God. Jesus acknowledges this in a faith shattering sermon in which he addresses the world and in which he also announces that he was mistaken in his belief in God and that we are all orphans.

Listen to this passage:

> I have been through the worlds, ascended to the suns and flown along the milky way through the wastes of heaven, but there is no God. I have descended as far as existence casts a shadow and looked into the abyss and cried: "Father, where art thou?" for he is not.

A final question of innocence is asked by the dead infants who fling themselves before Jesus: "Jesus, have we no father?" He answers with streaming tears, "We are all orphans, you and I, we have no Father . . . O blank, dumb nothingness."

How many people in the world, or for that matter in the church, have the feeling that the real thing in life is a "blank, dumb nothingness"?

Life and work have been robbed of meaning. We stand in a void that has no exit. What we believe has no lasting value, what we say is insignificant, what we do bears little resemblance to the truth within our lives. Ours is an age that seriously questions whether life or work has any meaning.

Perhaps this is precisely what Peter and the disciples were feeling at this point in the story in John's Gospel (John 21:1-7). They were at loose ends. They had returned home to their native Galilee, the quiet province by the shores of the sea from which Jesus had called them to follow him three years earlier. This was a sad homecoming for these fishermen turned itinerant disciples of the compelling yet gentle young man from Nazareth. Puzzled by the strange set of circumstances that led to his death on a cross, they were home to face the ridicule of the villagers who had watched them-beach their boats and leave their lucrative fishing business to follow this carpenter turned rabbi. Back home to Galilee they came, like soldiers from the wars, with their emotional and physical battle scars painfully raw.

The tragic venture had ended. Now they had to pick up the pieces of their lives. Nothing would ever be the same again. They would take nothing for that incredible interlude of life which they had shared with their Master. How real he had been; so human yet so like God. Then, in a brutal display of joint power by church and state, he was killed under circumstances that sickened them in their souls.

Misfortune, after all, is no respecter of persons. Dreams are unfulfilled; hopes fade; expectations disappoint; dear ones are lost. These fisherman had to choose to go on with life. As they had been called to become fishers of men, now they were called to choose life.

Life has a way of inviting us to do exactly that. Misfortune devastates and sometimes, like a Japanese bonsai tree, dwarfs our understanding of its meaning. See the parallel. These remarkable little dwarf trees are malformed by stunted grown. The process originated some four hundred fifty years ago when a gardener set a young pine tree in a shallow dish in one inch of soil. As the tree grew he trimmed each root and cut the branches back. When he died, his son tended the tree. This process was passed down through nineteen generations. This tree never outgrew its shallow dish. Today it stands in the Kuhara Gardens in Tokyo, a patriarch twenty inches high, three feet across, and much alive with its twisted top. Imagine that! Several hundred years old but only twenty inches high!

This little bonsai shouts a warning to us because the mind and soul can be dwarfed as well as a tree.

Peter and the disciples were traumatized when Jesus' life was cut short. They, like him, were the unhappy victims of the system. Now they are home trying to come to terms with themselves. It seemed the real thing to do. Still they remembered the sound of Jesus' voice, the look in his eyes, the lines in his face, and the touch of his hand and they hurt!

Jesus had come back to life and twice they had seen him but those moments were far too brief. It just wasn't like before! He had made them bold promises, but they couldn't comprehend. They heard him say, "I am on my way to the Father." Yes, the situation was vague and confusing. Time to settle down! Turn your back on the entire adventure! Take up the old life again!

So there they stood one night on the shore of the Sea of Galilee: Simon Peter, Nathanael, Thomas, James, John, and two others. Growing more and more perplexed, tired under the strain of waiting, Peter could take it no longer. "I'm going fishing!" he cried. That is all the others needed to hear. "We're going with you," they shouted.

They are on the Galilean Sea again at their long-deserted calling as fishermen. With hands on the oars throughout the night, they cast the net upon the water and watch it sink beneath the waves. Then, the Gospel writer sums up the setting in one terse sentence: "That night they caught nothing." Can you see them in that little boat beneath the Syrian sky, a thousand stars reflected on the water? Any fisherman will understand the disgust, the disappointment of Peter and that company who fished all night and caught nothing. They were tired, wet, and weary. Fishing—all night—for nothing.

This is a good place to speak to those of us today who are restless, impatient, at loose ends, and disenchanted with our life-long search, casting about in the sea of life, all the while catching nothing.

Our memory banks are filled with examples of people who, finding nothing, apparently chose to stop their world because they wanted to get off: America's sex goddess, Marilyn Monroe; Judy Garland, the child actress who became one of Hollywood's major draws; David Garroway, long-time television host of "The Today Show." Like thousands of others, they chose to end it all. They pursued the real thing in life yet it eluded them.

Who can ever forget the pathetic picture of the man called by many, at the time of his death, "the richest man in America"? Howard Hughes needlessly died of malnutrition and, the media reported, "without a genuine friend."

Life is passing by a multitude of folk who, though neither famous nor rich, have been searching for the real thing without ever finding it. In our consumer-oriented society in the Western world, we are preoccupied with things. We have assumed that basic values in life are to be found in material possessions. A recent exhibition of adult toys in the city in which I live drew tens of thousands of potential buyers. "Only the well-heeled can buy," one radio reporter said, "the others just look." We are rich in possessions and destitute in relationships.

Henry Wadsworth Longfellow said we are like:

> Ships that pass in the night, and speak to each other in
> passing,
> Only a signal shown and a distant voice in the darkness;
> So on the ocean of life, we pass and speak to another,
> Only a look and a voice, then darkness again and a
> silence.[1]

Some today are disenchanted with the church. They came searching, truly sincere about wanting to become a devout follower of Jesus Christ. For whatever reason, or no reason at all, they became disillusioned with the church and disappointed in Jesus, though they may not have seen him at all. The thing that they had hoped to find in the Christian life, for them turned out to be "no-thing" at all.

A newspaper in Brazil reported the story of a family living in one of the city's slums. There were six children and another on the way. They lived in a shack the size of a one-car garage. There was one piece of furnishing—a single mattress for the whole family. The headline of the article read, "God, where are you that you do not answer?"

Here is a young person who has been counseled "get your education" and after four or more years of college and graduate school, finds it impossible to get a job. He was squeezed out by our computer-run society. He might surmise he'd been fishing for nothing.

I see all kinds of people frantically searching for something better, plunging into all kinds of frenetic activity: some of it wonderful, a lot of it good, part of it utterly ridiculous. I marvel with disbelief at people following a new guru who formulates new dogma and doctrine by repudiating every belief and repealing every commandment ever known.

Like those disciples of old, these people are out on the sea of life, restless, frustrated, disillusioned, impatient, seeking, hoping, but seldom finding what they are looking for. Whether they're running away from life or running from Jesus, cynical about life or suspicious that it is all a hoax, they know the real thing has eluded them. Like those disciples, they have toiled all night and caught nothing. Many share the mood of the troubled Psalmist: "O that I knew where I might find him." They are utterly alone and feel sorry for themselves.

Thank God this is not the end of the story!

John says at the dawn's early light, after a night of utter frustration, the disillusioned fishermen saw a Man standing on the beach. He calls out, "Fellows, have you caught anything?" There were no excuses: "The fish aren't biting," or "We had the wrong bait." They answered him in one word, "No." "Cast the net on the right side of the boat, and you will catch some," he said.

Jim Fleming, that inimitable teacher in Jerusalem, told a group of us studying in Israel that in the early morning sunlight on the Sea of Galilee's western shore, one can easily spot a school of fish out in the deep. Jesus could see what the disciples could not see. So they threw their net into the water, it rose and spread out in a graceful circle and sank beneath he waves and almost at once it was filled with fish, so many the disciples could scarcely haul them in.

And John, the disciple whom Jesus loved, blurted out, "It is the Lord." Then Peter, in his usual impulsive manner, leapt overboard and swam for the shore, while the other disciples followed in the boat, dragging the net full of fish.

It was their Lord! And soon, beside a charcoal fire, they were having their breakfast. Cold and wet and tired they ate together beside the sea. They fed their bodies but of greater significance Jesus' presence nurtured their spirits. Over the water to that melancholy and disappointed boat of fishermen he called out and swift as lightning, their gloom was turned into gladness. Their uncomprehending slowness of heart was suddenly shot through with the reality: he is alive!

To recognize the risen Lord, to hear his voice, to respond to his call for these men is the real thing.

I recall hearing the story about Alfred Lord Tennyson meeting General William Booth, founder of the Salvation Army, one day while both were out walking. "General," said Tennyson, "what is the news this morning?" "The news, sir," replied Booth, "is that Christ died for our sins and rose for our justification!"

"Ah," replied the poet, "that is old news, and new news, and good news."

Analysts of the late twentieth century tell us we are the busiest and least contented people of all time. That message came home to me when I heard of a busy chief executive officer with a major Midwest corporation. He traveled frequently throughout the country taking care of his multiple executive responsibilities. One day his secretary received a telephone call from her frantic boss. He said, "I've just landed at the Minneapolis–St Paul airport. Why am I here?" We live in a hurry, we die in a hurry, we are buried in a hurry, and we are forgotten in a hurry.

We are afraid of the past and fearful of the future. Worry gnaws at our heart and our anxieties defy description. To borrow the words of one of Jesus' most familiar stories, we are choking on the worries and riches and pleasures of living and in the end we produce nothing. The real thing has passed us by. Or, have we been fishing in the wrong waters?

When will we discover that on the shore of life's restless sea, where we have spent too many nights, there stands a Man to whom we have not been listening and from whom we have been running?

He stands there waiting for those who hunger and thirst for meaning; who have searched and found nothing but emptiness in their quest; who faithfully have labored in some vineyard of the Lord and yet seem unrewarded; who bear a weary load of unconfessed guilt and what they consider unforgiven sin; who desperately are starving for love but even more desperately need to learn how to love.

He asks you the question he asked his disciples: "Have you caught anything in the midst of this search? Do you have what you want and what you need? Are you satisfied with your life?"

How shall we respond?

Shall we respond like the highly respected rich young

ruler who came running to Jesus to find out what is most important in life? Jesus loved him but the young man could not let go of his gods.

Or shall we respond like Zacchaeus, the tax collector, who was so thoroughly and heartily disliked by his fellow Jews for collaborating with the Romans? He told Jesus he'd give half of all he possessed to help the poor and promised to make fourfold restitution to anyone whom he had defrauded. Jesus said, "Today, salvation has come to this house."

Do you want to know Jesus better, to walk more closely beside him, to be numbered among his followers, to see him through the eyes of faith alive in our world, to receive the peace and power he offers? Would you like, in the words of Sir Richard Chichester, to "see him more clearly, love him more dearly, follow him more nearly"?

How tragic when we bottle it all up inside ourselves and search elsewhere for the real thing. What a priceless discovery to find that what makes sense in life is not the real thing but the Real Person. His name is Jesus and he gives us a new set of values that bring to life new ideals, new desires, and a whole new sense of obligation to God and man.

The Russian Orthodox Church recently celebrated a thousand years of Christianity in the Soviet Union. There was gripping evidence from those who visited Russia and the stories they related that despite seventy years of trying to foster atheism in Russia the church is very much alive there.

One of those stories is about a brilliant young Russian who confessed his new-found Christian faith before a Party leader. He knew his opportunity for education was now down the tube but he shared his new ideals: to love, not to hate; to have no enemies; to seek to overcome evil with good.

"Yes," the Communist leader said, "I understand, but

you must be realistic. These things you speak of are for your kingdom of God and it has not come yet."

"Sir," said the convert, "I realize it has not come for you or for the Soviet Union or for the world. But the kingdom of God has come for me!"

To Communists in Russia such faith is foolishness. To many in the Western world it seems impractical and old-fashioned. But without that quality of implicit faith in God and the reality of God's kingdom there is no security and no future. The great hope of our day is not in "containment" or in "co-existence," but in "regeneration."

The Christian gospel is the gospel of salvation for nations as well as for persons and the Christian life is a life—not of one who knows *about* Jesus, but who knows Jesus.

The *real* thing is found in our relationship with him. And the good news is: he is still saving people from their sins.

Then one of them, a lawyer, asked Him a question, testing Him, and saying,

"Teacher, which is the great commandment in the law?"

Jesus said to him, " 'You shall love the Lord your God with all your heart, with all your soul, and with all your mind.'

"This is the first and great commandment.

"And the second is like it: 'You shall love your neighbor as yourself.'

"On these two commandments hang all the Law and the Prophets" **(Matt. 22:35-40 NKJV).**

Listen to the Heartbeat!

My study in mid-town Detroit looks out over the headquarters of the world's largest corporation, General Motors. The automotive industry dominates the nation's fifth largest population center. To promote its chief product this industry's advertising promo is a catchy tune with a central jingle: "Listen to the heartbeat of America." Detroit put America on wheels so I'm confident many feel that the heartbeat of the nation *is* a sporty car or truck. Certainly, this seductive ad would have us believe it. I question such advertising assertions! God save us if the heartbeat of America is an automobile.

I want to believe that at the heart of American people is the central teaching of Jesus. It is, in brief, the summation of the law: *love for God and for neighbor.* Jesus was not the first to sum up God's requirements. In the passage from Matthew it is the lawyer who gives the summary; Jesus accepts and concurs with his response. It matters little who says it or who said it first. What matters is that 613 commandments computed by the rabbis have been gathered into one. We are to love God with all our heart, soul, strength, and mind and our neighbor as ourself. As Paul would write later to the church at Rome, "Love is the fulfilling of the law" (Rom. 13:10 NKJV). And love is the heartbeat of the Christian message.

Twenty centuries of Christian history have given us a number of models of Christian love. A Methodist model whose heartbeat continues to thrill me is John Wesley. Do you know the Wesleyan story? Have you heard of the experience that warmed his heart and helped save a nation?

Eighteenth-century England was in a time of vast spiritual decay. The depth, apathy, and shame to which organized religion had sunk begs description. England, in large measure, was a gin-soaked, dissolute country, full of destitution and depravity. The people were without hope and without help.

It was a time of greed, lust, and unbridled passion. The power of the Christian religion was largely broken. It was a roaring, bustling, brutal entertainment-seeking age. There was a great deal of violent crime. Bear baiting was a common sport. Boxing, even among women, was a customary pastime. Cockfighting, gambling, drinking, and attending public hangings were popular amusements.

The church had a kept clergy who, either out of laziness or indifference, ceased to proclaim the Word of God. No longer capable of a religious fervor, the church was also no longer a threat to the tyranny, corruption, injustice, and sin of the day. In short the church was failing to care for the people and reduced God to the status quo.

But God had a surprise in store for England and the church!

On a sunny June day in 1703 the fifteenth baby was born to a family who lived in a rambling old rectory already overflowing in the Lincolnshire market town of Epworth. Little John Benjamin Wesley with blue eyes, auburn hair, and long nose came to a desperately poor couple. For three generations his ancestors had been gentle folk by birth, scholars by training, and clergymen by choice. His father was Samuel Wesley, an Anglican clergyman. His mother, Susanna, would bear nineteen children in twenty-one years. What a remarkable woman! While her husband remained locked in his study writing ponderous books (all of which were still-born) she managed the household and nurtured the children. Only nine of the nineteen children lived beyond childhood but these nine learned respect for their mother. Susanna herself said that the children "were taught to fear the rod and to cry softly" and "that most odious noise of the crying of children was rarely heard"[1] in her house. Again I say, Susanna Wesley was an extraordinary mother.

The children were taught to pray the Lord's Prayer as soon as they could talk. Each child learned the alphabet on his or her fifth birthday. Since there was no school for the small children to attend, Susanna taught them to read. The Bible was their first reader and the opening chapter of Genesis was their first lesson. School was held in the Epworth rectory every week day from nine to twelve and two to five.

One recorded incident from his boyhood could well be one of the most important of his life. On a cold February night the rectory was torched by hostile parishioners. The thatched roof structure was totally consumed fifteen minutes after the fire was discovered.

In terror the family awakened the children, scurrying out of the flaming inferno only to discover that five-year-old John was missing. He was still asleep in his attic bedroom. His father dropped to his knees, commending his little one to God's mercy. John, meanwhile, was aroused by the crackling fire, pushed a chest to the window, suddenly appearing amid the flames enveloping the blazing roof. A human ladder lifted him to safety an instant before the roof caved in. So etched in his memory was that moment that Wesley vividly reflected on it a half century later, composing his own epitaph, the "brand plucked from the burning."

At age eleven he entered Charterhouse School in London as a charity pupil. He excelled in his studies.

Daily he ran three laps around the playground to preserve his health. At age eighty, hale and hearty, he attributed his robust vitality to is boyhood discipline at Charterhouse.

As a commoner, he received a scholarship in 1720 to Oxford's Christ Church College. The students there were keener on drinking and gambling than study and work. The complacent dons took their salary and dodged their duty.

But John, a true son of Susanna, designed a program for systematizing his work and followed it methodically. While his letters home during his early years at Oxford didn't speak much of religion, they did reveal an eager, growing mind. By graduation he began to consider the ministry.

His father welcomed the idea but urged him to spend some time studying ancient languages before entering holy orders. His mother disagreed. She wrote, "It is an unhappiness, almost peculiar to our family, that your father and I seldom think alike."[2] She urged him to begin the study of theology immediately. He followed her advice. From this time on, his letters home were filled with discussions of religion.

Wesley was ordained a deacon in 1725 and a presbyter in 1728. He served briefly as an assistant to his father but spurned Samuel's desire for his son to succeed him as rector at Epworth.

As a fellow at Lincoln College he was a grim high churchman. The general rules he drew up for himself governed his conduct. He resolved to employ all his spare time in religion, to keep all holy days, to avoid busybodies and drunkards, vain and light company, all freedom with women, lusts and impure thoughts. Likewise he resolved to shirk no duty, begin each work with prayer, and to give up laughter and useless conversation.

He was miserable!

Rising at four in the morning, he fasted regularly,

worked every waking minute, visited prisoners, as well as inmates of the poorhouse and the madhouse, taught ignorant children, and daily partook of the Lord's Supper. His carefully prepared sermons drew no crowds, influenced no lives, touched no consciences, warmed no hearts.

A spiritual prisoner to the law and in bondage to a theology of good works, he was, in his own words, "an almost Christian."

Is it surprising, then, to find him on a ship with his brother, Charles, bound for America as a missionary to the Indians? Before sailing for Georgia, Wesley notes his chief motive, "Our end . . . was . . . to save our souls."[3]

On that journey across the Atlantic, which lasted fifty-one days, the Wesley brothers met the Moravians–German Christians who had an intense courage arising out of absolute faith. John was terribly frightened by a series of storms and asked the calm and serene Moravians, "Were you not afraid?" "I thank God, no," was the reply. He was told not even the women and children were afraid because they "are not afraid to die."[4] This experience was to profoundly influence John Wesley.

In the Colony he met great personal distress. He was angered by the drunkenness and apathy of the Indians. The Georgians, released debtors from English prisons, hated this stern Anglican priest. One woman tried to seduce him and then threatened him with a loaded pistol and a pair of scissors.

Wesley returned to England in 1737, a failure in his own eyes. A year later he wrote of that moment, "I was not a Christian then." Out of his own agony he preached sermons that were received with anger.

At the home of a friend he met Peter Böhler, a young German theologian on his way to the new world as a missionary. For the next three months Wesley and Böhler shared constantly, arguing and wrestling over matters of faith.

Böhler wrote his mentor in Germany, "I travelled with the two brothers . . . the elder, John, is a good-natured man . . . willing to be taught. . . . Our mode of believing . . . is so easy to Englishmen, that they cannot reconcile themselves to it; . . . they justify themselves . . . and try to prove their faith, by their works and thus so plague and torment themselves that they are at heart very miserable."[5]

How right were Böhler's words! Wesley was miserable. He had been trying to gain salvation by works; he was trying to make himself worthy of God's love. He would learn that salvation comes, not by works, but by faith. It is the grace of God that is our hope, not the work of men and women.

Wesley found this hard to understand but he thought about it constantly and began to preach it. To his surprise, people began to respond to his preaching more than they ever had before. Still he was dissatisfied.

On May 24, 1738, a new heartbeat would break into the life of Wesley. At five in the morning he tells us that he opened his New Testament and his eyes fell upon these words: "Whereby are given unto us exceeding great and precious promises: that by these, ye might be partakers of the divine nature" (II Pet. 1:4 KJV). Later he opened it again, and these words spoke to him: "Thou art not far from the kingdom of God" (Mark 12:34 KJV).

In the afternoon he went to a service at St. Paul's Cathedral, where the choir sang: "Out of the depths have I cried unto thee, O Lord. Lord, hear my voice. . . . Let Israel hope in the Lord: for with the Lord there is mercy, and with him is plenteous redemption. And he shall redeem Israel from all his iniquities" (Ps. 130:1-2a, 7-8 KJV). The anthem matched his mood at that moment. "Lord, hear my voice," sang the choir and surely John Wesley continued that prayer in the silence of his heart as he left St. Paul's.

That evening, tired and miserable, he ambled down a cobblestone street called Aldersgate for a Moravian prayer meeting. He confesses, "I went very unwillingly."[6] He took a seat and a man began reading Martin Luther's Preface to the Epistle to the Romans. The great reformer speaks of the Holy Spirit "making new hearts, exhilarating us, exciting and inflaming our heart that it may do those things willingly of love which the law commands."

Wesley listened to every word and God was waiting for that listening heart. What God was working in Wesley's heart was infinitely more significant than the works Wesley was doing for God. Suddenly something came alive in the soul of Wesley. In his heart he felt it for the first time! It warmed him through and through. Later that night he wrote in his Journal, a calm summary of the happening of that extraordinary moment:

> About a quarter before nine, while he was describing the change which God works in the heart through faith in Christ, I felt my heart strangely warmed. I felt that I did trust in Christ, Christ alone for salvation, and an assurance was given me, that he had taken away *my* sins, even *mine*, and saved *me* from the law of sin and death. I began to pray with all my might for those who had in a more especial manner despitefully used me and persecuted me. I then testified openly to all there what I now first felt in my heart.[7]

At last he found the key to unlock the door. He had been a believer. Now he could love and obey. He had been a servant, now he was a son! How simple! *Believe, love, obey!* The assurance—*now* he had it! His prayer had been answered. In a flash it had come to him as it had to Paul. His heart was bursting with a new love. John Wesley then and there gave himself to God. His sins had been taken away. He was from now on God's son. *His part was to believe, to love, and to obey.*

A heartwarming happened that night. A conversion, some might call it. The label matters little; the experience matters much.

When he left the prayer meeting he had the same heart but the heart had a different beat! He hastened to tell the glorious news to his brother Charles, ill at his home, minutes away. Charles understood instantly because he had experienced three days earlier a changed heartbeat. Charles quickly shared a newly written hymn prompted by the experience. He read it to John and the two of them, with their friends joining in, sang it for the first time:

> Where shall my wondering soul begin?
> How shall I all to heaven aspire?
> A slave redeemed from death and sin,
> A brand plucked from eternal fire,
> How shall I equal triumphs raise,
> Or sing my great deliverer's praise?
>
> Or how shall I the goodness tell,
> Father, which thou to me has showed?
> That I, a child of wrath and hell,
> I should be called a child of God,
> Should know, should feel my sins forgiven,
> Blest with this antepast of heaven.
>
> Come, O my guilty brethren, come,
> Groaning beneath your load of sin!
> His bleeding heart shall make you room;
> His open side shall take you in.
> He calls you now, invites you home:
> Come, O my guilty brethren, come!

Methodism, I believe, was born that night.

In the hearts of John and Charles they had believed. Now they knew their sins forgiven! They gave themselves wholly to God, determined from that moment to love and to obey.

The two Wesleys became God's revolutionaries. England began to hear a new heartbeat.

After their heartwarming experience they began to preach in ways that alarmed the vicars and churchwardens. Rough and ignorant people, and even criminals, flocked in great crowds to hear them. Their message was so simple, so direct, so convincing that multitudes cried out in their agony of shame with repentance. The two Wesleys and George Whitefield, the cross-eyed son of an innkeeper and friend from Holy Club days at Oxford, drew spectacular crowds. John Wesley preached about God seeking his children and passed on the steps to commitment: *believe, love, obey.*

The clergy were outraged. These unwashed hordes packed their churches weeping and crying out to God as the Wesleys preached convincing sermons and gave persuasive altar calls. In church after church changed lives were evident: thieves became honest, drunks sober, brutal and cruel men became kind and gentle.

The church, repulsed by such a revolting display of unforgivable enthusiasm, closed pulpit after pulpit to these zealous young men. Forced to go into the open air when parish churches slammed shut their doors, Wesley announced, "I look upon all the world as my parish."[8] He became better known by sight than any Englishman, kings and queens included. This preaching friar of the eighteenth century would preach over forty thousand sermons, an average of fifteen a week, and crisscross England at least a quarter of a million miles. The deep devotion, selfless service, high purpose and dauntless courage of John Wesley changed the course of eighteenth-century England.

Listen to the heartbeat! In this heartbeat one finds the significant factor in the new life and spirit breathed into England and which now touches tens of millions of Christians around the world.

Where shall my wondering soul begin? It begins when we want to get rid of everything evil in our hearts and we are determined to move beyond belief to love and obey.

In loving obedience, Wesley founded England's first free medical dispensary. To give employment to the poor, he set up spinning and knitting shops. A Benevolent Loan Fund was established to help finance new business enterprises. The Strangers' Friend Society gave relief to "the poor, sick and friendless strangers." He gave away $200,000—royalties from his books—and limited himself to $150 a year for personal expenses. Once he said he'd give people the privilege of calling him a robber if he owned more than $50 at the time of his death.

John Wesley lived to be eighty-eight. On his deathbed he called out, "Where is my sermon on the love of God? Take it and spread it abroad. Give it to everyone."

His burial was in keeping with his life's commitment. His instructions were followed to the letter: burial in nothing more costly than wool; whatever remained in his dresser and pockets to be given to his Methodist followers. As a protest against needless funeral expense, he directed in his will "no hearse, no coach, no pomp." He ordered instead that six poor unemployed men be hired at one pound each to bear his body to its grave.

Wesley's last will and testament is stamped with his seal. I have seen that seal. On it are three words. What are they? *Believe, love, obey!*

Listen to the heartbeat!

"Glory to God in the highest,
and on earth peace among men with whom he is
pleased!" **(Luke 2:14)**.

"Peace I leave with you; my peace I give to you; not as the
world gives do I give to you. Let not your hearts be troubled,
neither let them be afraid" **(John 14:27)**.

And how shall they preach, except they be sent? as it is written,
How beautiful are the feet of them that preach the gospel of peace,
and bring glad tidings of good things! **(Rom. 10:15 KJV)**.

Every Missile Is Aimed at Jesus!

The true role of prophetic, biblical religion is to speak God's message. Yet it is a major tragedy and a minor irony that the Christian Church experiences more dissension and debate over the Christian responsibility for peace, the meaning of peace, and the way to peace than perhaps any other subject. In thirty-five years as a Methodist pastor I have witnessed more conflict, the sharpest divisions, the deepest feelings, the bitterest strife on the matter of war and peace than any other subject.

As long as the focus is on peace of mind, or peace as a distant goal or ideal, no one gets upset. Most people seem to hear the words of Jesus about peace as soothing promises. They prefer to think of his peace in terms of John Greenleaf Whittier's moving hymn:

> Drop thy still dews of quietness,
> Till all our strivings cease;
> Take from our souls the strain and stress,
> And let our ordered lives confess
> The beauty of thy peace.

Or they underscore, that we have known little peace in the world. A widely read writer pointed out a quarter of a century ago that in the fifty-six centuries of recorded history, the world has known only 292 years of peace. He says that 14,513 wars have been fought since

3600 B.C. and almost one and a quarter *billion* people have died either in combat or as a result of war. One may not be able to verify the accuracy of these figures but they reveal one startling fact: *we have known "wars and rumors of wars" more than we have known peace.*

The United Nations designated 1986 as the Year of Peace. Yet when the history of the year was recorded the tragic news told of thirty-six wars and armed conflicts around the world. Some three to five million people died because of those wars. Some Year of Peace!

Despite these grim statistics I remain optimistic!

Jesus promises peace in the gospel. "Peace I leave with you; my peace I give to you" (John 14;27*a*). But he goes on to say, "Not as the world gives do I give to you" (John 14:27*b*).

I believe Jesus Christ came into the world to show the world the way to peace. I believe God through Christ Jesus ultimately is the One who reigns and who will reign and that the ways of peace will prevail. However, there is a price for peace. As a people of the resurrection, we know there is no shortcut to Easter which bypasses Gethsemane and Calvary. Peacemaking is costly.

The tragic fact is that the Christian Church has not spoken with a clear witness and convincing voice on the matter of war and peace. We have sounded our trumpets, all right, but as one has put it, "The sound it emits reminds one of nothing so much as a beginning musician's first attempt to play a horn . . . an awful alternation between unbelievable silence and unbearable sound."

Our failure does not acquit us, however, because we are called to be obedient and faithful to the mandate laid upon us as disciples of Christ. We are *to show* the ways of peace, *to proclaim* the ways of peace, *to be peacemakers* not just peace talkers. This call is true for the Christian in all areas of life—not just war and peace. All relationships within life are covered by this summons. Peace is attainable because God has shown us in Christ Jesus it is possible. The resurrection of Jesus from the dead—the triumph of God over evil and injustice—is the hope that gives me faith in the possibility of peace!

There is a beautiful story about the last days of one of England's tireless workers for peace. George Lansbury spent all his mature life wrestling with the knotty problems that lead to war. He lived through the World War I and when he died, the guns of the World War II were echoing in Europe and the Pacific. To the Christians and British realists, it seemed that he had thrown away his forty years of struggle. A dear friend asked him how much nearer he thought peace was as a result of his effort. George Lansbury replied, "Forty years nearer."

Jesus was born in the midst of a society that was based on power and militarism. Jesus' ethic was not popular. The same ethic is not popular for many today. "Blessed are the peacemakers," Jesus said, "for they shall be called the children of God" (Matt. 5:9 KJV). A paraphrase of that verse puts it, "Happy are those who work for peace." The emphasis is on the working, the making of peace. That point is often missed. Jesus did not say, "Blessed are the *peace-lovers*, the peaceable." Jesus' word for us is, "Blessed are the *peacemakers*"; "happy are those who *work* for peace." To actively respond to his call—not sit quietly by and hope for the best—is to be a reconciler among people and nations.

Still he calls us to be his disciples. I'm excited when I see people's lives take on the way of Christ and the way of peace. One gets a glimpse of this when a person like Gandhi adopts the ways of Jesus for peace making and becomes a witness to the nation-state of India and the world.

One of the most courageous moves of the twentieth century was the journey of Anwar Sadat who dared to go to Jerusalem and say to the Jewish Parliament, "I come in the name of peace." Then the Egyptian

President sat down with Golda Meir, and the two shared pictures of their children and grandchildren. One man boldly crossed that dividing line between two peoples, two cultures, two ways of life at loggerheads for two thousand years.

We need to take steps that lead to peace. Pastors and laity are not tactical experts but when initiatives for peace are taken, we should show our willingness to risk in order to build a basis of trust!

In the history of the church there have been times when we have been willing to proclaim the Good News but unwilling to take upon ourselves the burden of risk-taking.

One of the more shameful aspects of American church history concerns the great evangelist, George White-field. He was a man whom God called and equipped and to whom God gave the power of the gospel that was awe-inspiring! Whitefield was America's first truly great evangelist. It was said one could hear Whitefield preaching for one mile and singing for two.

At one stage of his ministry he preached to over 80 percent of the people who lived in the colonies. He proclaimed the gospel with fervor and was in the forefront of the religious revival that swept through New England and into the South. Ben Franklin admired him as he did no other preacher.

When Whitefield was in the colonies, he was heart sick about the growing slave traffic. On one occasion he spoke to a few slave owners about it and received such rebuke and hardship that he never again addressed the issue of slavery.

Whitefield continued to proclaim the gospel of Jesus and the new life that Jesus offered but he refused to attack slavery. Today, as revisionists rewrite the history of that era, some say that one man held the key and could have changed the course of American history. If George Whitefield had hit hard on the slave issue, proclaiming release in Jesus' name, he might have brought freedom to the slaves. He had the power, the respect, and the authority to speak to that wickedness and bondage, but he failed to address it! Generation after generation of blacks suffered incredibly. The Civil War was a bloody chapter, and racism is a cancer upon the soul of America to this very day.

It is never enough to proclaim the Good News. Christians must be risk-takers. It is never enough to pray for peace if we are unwilling to take the initiative, to show our willingness to take first steps, to lose ourselves for the sake of the gospel in order to bring about unity and reconciliation between peoples and nations.

Yet, God's way to peace seems such an outrage to thinking human beings. "Love your enemies, do good to them which hate you" (Luke 6:27 KJV). Bless those who persecute you! Do good to those who try to destroy you? Give double to those who try to exploit you? You've got to be kidding! Is this what faithful discipleship is all about?

Faith is a gift, an audacious gift. It is the ability to walk in God's outrageous, upside-down paths when any sane person knows it makes no sense at all. Such faith moves on to obey.

One of my favorite Old Testament stories about such faith is told in II Kings 6. The Arameans are terrorizing Israel. This was not provocation or mild harassment. It was not a case of kids throwing stones or rocks. I am talking about marauding troops surging in on innocent civilians. I'm talking about the expropriation of crops and homes.

Elisha tells the king not to do battle with the enemy. Such foolishness has, of course, its consequences. The army moves in and is about to occupy the land. God blinds the invading troops. Elisha goes out and tricks the blinded Arameans into following him. By the time their sight returns, they're in the center of Samaria, the capital, surrounded by the Israelite king and his troops.

"Shall I destroy them?" asks the king of Israel, delighted at the chance to kill these marauders once and for all. "No," replies Elisha. "Give them food and water—and then let them go." How outrageous, absolutely outrageous! Take these enemies, treat them like a visiting monarch, and let them go?

But the king obeyed because he believed the command came from God. Such is the faith that we all need. "And so the king prepared a great feast for his enemies, and they ate and drank, and then went back to their master" (II Kings 6:23). *And the Aramean raids on Israel ceased.*

Every time I read that story my hopes for peace are buoyed. What a portrait of how God invites us, sinners all, to the great feast in his commonwealth of the world. Do we really desire peace with those who oppress us? Do we seek to be free of international terrorism? God's invitation is downright ludicrous: call a feast, treat your enemy as your guest! "If your enemy is hungry, feed him; if he is thirsty, give him drink; for by so doing you will heap burning coals upon his head" (Rom. 12:20). Paul is right. The best way to deal with an enemy is not to burn him up but melt him down. The prophet Elisha would simply have invited this nation's enemies to a rollicking good state party at 1600 Pennsylvania Avenue. But *our* response to the arms race is to rattle our sabers and build an ever-larger stockpile of bargaining warheads!

America needs to export wonder-working values instead of wonder-working weapons. We are all things to all people because we like it that way. Have we been seduced more by a love of power than by the power of love? Have we, as Christians, become more concerned about *projecting* an image than we are in *reflecting* an Image?

Christians are the alternative community to a society based on power. All around the world America is seen as being on the defensive. We need to take the offensive, seize the initiative, show our willingness to take those first steps. Christians are called to be the Lord's vanguard. If we don't take the initiative, who will? If Christians cannot model the ways of Jesus for the world, the way to reconciliation that bridges communities and brings meaning to people's lives, who will? Let the grass roots effort at peacemaking begin with us.

President Dwight D. Eisenhower's insight of years ago is finding more and more response today. Ike said, "Some day the people of the world are going to want peace so much that the governments are going to have to get out of their way and let them have it." It's beginning to happen.

Increasing numbers of Christians and other Americans are visiting Eastern Europe and the Soviet Union as a concrete step in peacemaking on the citizen level. Some officials say these people-to-people efforts are not significant; only government-to-government exchanges are important. These visits may be only drops in a bucket. But enough drops in a bucket will produce a bucketful. That's the purpose! Drop after drop of reaching out to officials, church people, ordinary folk helps to create a shift in our awareness and perceptions. Attitudes can change; trust can be built on both sides, spreading like leaven across the globe.

Eleven years separate us from the third millennium of the Christian era. How will the world step over this threshold? I dare to believe it will be in response to a strong and clear message from the church: "The God of life calls us all: turn away from the path of death and choose life."

It was at the grass roots that the song of peace was first heard. The Christian era began with a heavenly host praising God saying, "Glory to God in the highest, and on earth peace among men with whom he is pleased" (Luke 2:14). How those terror-struck shepherds under the heel of Rome must have welcomed that song! It was not in Caesar's palace or Herod's court that the angelic choir sang. On a rock-strewn hillside outside a cave the ordinary common working folk heard that chorus. A promise of peace on earth.

Near the end of Jesus' earthly ministry he promised his troubled disciples a gift. "Peace I leave with you; my peace I give to you" (John 14:27).

One who was a recipient of that gift of peace would write years later to the church at Rome, "How beautiful are the feet of them that preach the gospel of peace, and bring glad tidings of good things!" (Rom. 10:15 KJV).

We are the inheritors of the angelic song, this gift from Jesus, and word of affirmation from Paul. Will the world survive the threat of nuclear destruction in the eleven years that separate us from the third millennium of the Christian era?

Let us dare to believe and pray, work and risk to convince the church and the world, "The God of life calls us all; turn away from the path of death and choose life."

Frederick Buechner has asked our generation a searching question:

> What are we defending, our enemies and we? Well, we are defending our homes, our children. We are defending the welfare of our people and the traditions of our fathers. And so of course are they. The tragic irony, of course, is that all these precious things we and our enemies are both defending are threatened by nothing so much as by the very process we use to defend them.
>
> A nation has only so much money to spend, so much time, so much ingenuity, to spend, and as the years go by we and our enemies are both spending so much of all of these things on the great instruments of death that we have less and less to spend on the things that make our lives worth even living let alone worth dying for: less and less to spend on hospitals and housing and schools, on feeding our children, on halting the decay of our cities, on works of compassion. We are defending our very lives as nations, we believe, but what happens to the quality of that life, the heart and genius of that life, when such matters as these are neglected?[1]

I don't know about you, but I am deeply moved by his soul-searching comment.

I was equally moved a couple of years ago when I learned of two bedridden, invalid sisters. Facing death, confined to four walls, they decided to give the rest of their lives and their money to influence Christians and politicians on this issue. Now, they spend their days writing letters and circulating petitions. They also send a picture. One is an artist who has painted a picture of a mushroom cloud with a figure on a cross at its center. It bears the caption: *"Every missile in the world is pointed at Jesus."*

And the message is unmistakable: Anything you did for one of my brothers here, however humble, you did for me (Matt. 25:40*b* NEB).

Every missile is aimed at Jesus? I dare you! Think about it!

Notes

Chapter 1

1. Anthony Padovano, *Free to Be Faithful* (Paramus, N.J.: Paulist Press, 1972), p. 49.

Chapter 2

1. William Barclay, *The Gospel of Luke*, the Daily Study Bible series (Philadelphia: Westminster Press, 1957), p. 206.
2. Keith Miller, *The Taste of New Wine* (Waco, Tex.: Word Books, 1965), pp. 38-39.
3. Ibid., p. 39.

Chapter 3

1. Helmut Thielicke, *The Waiting Father* (New York: Harper & Row, 1957), p. 46.
2. George A. Buttrick, *The Parables of Jesus* (Grand Rapids, Mich.: Baker Book House, 1973), p. 139.

Chapter 4

1. William Barclay, *The Gospel of Luke*, the Daily Study Bible series (Philadelphia: Westminster Press, 1957), p. 228.
2. Ibid., p. 229.
3. Richard B. Wilke, "Challenging a Church Out of Focus," *Good News*, September/October 1986, pp. 10-16.
4. James M. Efird, *End-Times* (Nashville: Abingdon Press, 1986), p. 13.
5. John L. McKenzie, *The New Testament Without Illusion* (New York, N.Y.: Crossroad Publishing Co., 1982), p. 74.

Chapter 5

1. Harry Emerson Fosdick, *The Meaning of Prayer* (Chicago: Follett Publishing Co., 1949, 1962), p. 130.
2. William Barclay, *Everyday Prayers* (New York: Harper & Row, 1959), p. 13.
3. *The Journal of John Wesley.*
4. Gerald Kennedy, *While I'm on My Feet* (Nashville: Abingdon Press, 1963), pp. 58-59.

Chapter 6

1. Lloyd C. Douglas, *The Robe* (Boston: Houghton Mifflin Co., 1942), p. 68.
2. From *The Unutterable Beauty, the Collected Poetry of G. A. Studdert-Kennedy* (New York: Harper & Brothers, 1936), p. 117.

Chapter 8

1. Albert Schweitzer, *The Quest of the Historical Jesus* (London: A. & C. Black, 1922) p. 401.

Chapter 9

1. William Barclay, *The Gospel of Luke*, the Daily Study Bible series (Philadelphia: Westminster Press, 1957), p. 143.
2. Aldous Huxley, *Tomorrow and Tomorrow and Tomorrow and Other Essays* (New York: Harper & Row, 1972). p. 7.

Chapter 10

1. From *Tales of a Wayside Inn: The Theologian's Tale: Elizabeth.* Pt. iv.

Chapter 11

1. *The Journal of John Wesley.*
2. James Richard Joy, *John Wesley's Awakening* (New York: The Methodist Book Concern, 1937), pp. 35-36.
3. *The Journal.*
4. Ibid.
5. Wesley Bready, *England, Before and After Wesley* (Tampa, Fla.: Russell Publications, 1971), p. 191.

6. *The Journal.*
7. Ibid.
8. Ibid.

Chapter 12

1. Frederick Buechner, *A Room Called Remember* (New York: Harper & Row, 1984), p. 76.